The Absence of Zero

The Absence of Zero

R. Kolewe

44 quartets & 34 interruptions in 16 parts

Book*hug Press
Toronto 2021

Library and Archives Canada Cataloguing in Publication

Title: The absence of zero : 44 quartets & 34 interruptions in 16 parts / R. Kolewe.

Other titles: Absence of 0

Names: Kolewe, R. (Ralph), 1957— author.

Description: First edition. | Poem.

Identifiers: Canadiana (print) 20210289287 | Canadiana (ebook) 20210289295

    ISBN 9781771667265 (softcover)

    ISBN 9781771667272 (EPUB)

    ISBN 9781771667289 (PDF)

Classification: LCC PS8621.O47 A64 2021 | DDC C811/.6—dc23

Image credits

Page 2: Albrecht Dürer, *Melencolia I*, 1514, Metropolitan Museum of Art, New York City. Public domain image downloaded from their website.

Page 443: Albrecht Dürer, *Saint Jerome in His Study*, 1514, Honolulu Museum of Art, Honolulu. Public domain image download from Wikipedia Commons.

The production of this book was made possible through the generous assistance of the Canada Council for the Arts and the Ontario Arts Council. Book*hug Press also acknowledges the support of the Government of Canada through the Canada Book Fund and the Government of Ontario through the Ontario Book Publishing Tax Credit and the Ontario Book Fund.

Book*hug Press acknowledges that the land on which we operate is the traditional territory of many nations, including the Mississaugas of the Credit, the Anishnabeg, the Chippewa, the Haudenosaunee, and the Wendat peoples. We recognize the enduring presence of many diverse First Nations, Inuit, and Métis peoples and are grateful for the opportunity to meet, work, and learn on this territory.

Book*hug Press

In memory of

Christina Baillie (1958–2019)

&

Ward McBurney (1962–2019)

$$R^{\rho}{}_{\sigma\mu\nu} = \partial_{\mu}\Gamma^{\rho}{}_{\nu\sigma} - \partial_{\nu}\Gamma^{\rho}{}_{\mu\sigma} + \Gamma^{\rho}{}_{\mu\lambda}\Gamma^{\lambda}{}_{\nu\sigma} - \Gamma^{\rho}{}_{\nu\lambda}\Gamma^{\lambda}{}_{\mu\sigma}$$

4

& if I interrupt myself
again or for the first time—

0.0.0.0

The line moves. The shadow moves.
Early winters almost remembered. Not exactly
how to empty out the teaching
where relativistic effects are important:

filling time with pages instead.
Not yet & then after there is a word.
A family of curves, coastline doubling back to television snow.
Orion first. Exploitation

of electrical demand / power factors / naive presence —
without clocks how small time is church bells & canonical hours
in the induced topology. A map, a proper map,
so the submanifold may not intersect itself.

Uncertain if there are figures without boundaries,
leave pages blank, nothing uncovered
distance scattering error quantum error & so
beginning with unrecognized constellations —

0.0.0.1

Quick motion all corners in this cottage or gentrified row house
love & strife or is it love & disease or theft & early transcendentals.
Then its translation reads
a chain of alternatives unchosen / losses

reminding myself that I can delete this rewrite substantially—
at this old pine table quiet street slight wind
recollection returns, breathing becomes difficult again, wearying,
relative to its centre of mass & also relative to

having lost my way in connections but not connected.
Dreaming a different garden, shady, an oak & an owl
at once without certainty leaving me
if you are real or the children's voices

parallel transport to covariant derivative to geodesic.
Without memory rust or other words
aureole, variable, wind again, warm skin.
Set them down on the red chair at the top of the stairs.

0.0.0.2

Lane warm lit windows in the twilight woods torn clouds thin moon.
Light shifts. Light slants, conciliate or another word
being tilted in another direction
how thought comes into mind or memory & arcs out.

Wind bending the trees in the east burning information.
The cat sleeping, dreaming under the desk lamp where it's warm.
That would say each independent & whole
no garden voices words not quite heard correctly

under fading dust wrappers sky blue cloth fine with no markings or
    annotations to return to
good as reading great books copying lines down from the radio who has a
    radio—
with an undertone of ecstatic grammar.
Flew off silent in the cool of the morning now

should be or is it will have been
unrecognized names wasted teleology or a diary
pencil burin Swiss micrometer no words but a tone of voice that fades—
& after that what does zero mean.

0.0.0.3

By hand, imperfect concentration but applying it directly.
The neighbour's porch light on across the street.
Change in a field relative to the parallel
moonglow on blackout streets. Bodies & body parts. Erased.

The angular velocities of stationary observers are constrained.
Then an airliner, & a car horn,
the trees filling in the patterned sidewalk & quiet I get distracted.
Lacework of quotation. Another notebook. Time. Weather.

In the absence of a metric
with sunrise moonrise later
& these aren't my ruins to stumble over
or fast & then clocks & wind.

Not being able to touch this —
I would like a chalkboard to write on to erase time & again.
The unkempt awkward folding flap of wings after they land
is memory & you can forget something never remembered.

0.0.1.0

Like writing by hand but nobody's hand no the hand of electricity—
At this old pine table quiet street slight wind
last. These indices are symmetric
in unusual coordinates an artifact of viewpoint centrifugal

having lost my way in connections but not connected
more difficult than coming through nothing
gives the time required to travel
at the trestle table beside the high windows the fox & the lion—

& after that what does zero mean.
A chain of alternatives unchosen / losses
after strife or love swerve to silent
astronomy answer questions with evasion anything like truth.

What you want is explanation & at some time or point
a net of geodesics not causation self-similarity.
That time seems impossible, unrepeatable now.
Apples dried up into sketches.

0.0.1.1

So a list of losses at canonical hours
ending with time beginning
thick paint, without a determined design watching
or coloured in bright tropic orange green or dark blue —

to the mark chalk or ash or plumb line blue
is also a unique function
a positive constant of order unity given by
the gravitational deflection of light &

one might expect the occasional close
delusion of black & white.
Wet streets after rain meeting no one
at once without certainty leaving me

with the measured annual variations of
an epiphany. How to answer that? With leaving,
a chain of alternatives unchosen / losses
distance scattering error quantum error & so —

0.0.1.2

The time after
exists without you.
Forget. These aren't your memories anyway.
A snowball thrown into the Grand Canyon by an 8-year-old.

At least I'll fill this page always one more thing,
geodesic grain & ashes of words mainly numbers
there are too many sheets of paper not
the same & not the same a path of scatters—

there are too many sheets of paper.
Do I refuse recollection or is there nothing to remember?
Who lives there now? A character from an old book.
Branches unrecognized decisions different lives

still down your tools compass square green mechanical
galaxies with distances greater than
no path retraced eyes closed wanting not
so loss creates & holds what is lost.

0.0.1.3

Argument or conspiracy, perhaps endearments, seduction —
the ashes of stories memories of fire & the sound of fire
is about to break the time
this undertaking requires a knowledge of.

Over years & so the rose garden & everybody knows the ruined chapels
    country houses broken cities
& the comfort of banality more tempting not fire —
Sublime melancholy! Is that the remainder?
Not fire but its deep blue core.

No garden voices words not quite heard correctly.
Elliptical, allusive vague light
unrecognized names wasted teleology or a diary
like writing by hand but nobody's hand no the hand of electricity —

as a function of proper time measured on
loss creates & holds what is lost.
Sit with my back to the tree leaning looking up
words instead of feeling or real thought.

0.0.2.0

A positive constant of order unity given by
midday. Unopened books unfinished doubt
salamander quick in the flames the coals ash jewelled eyes—
by hand (time & weather) the sky.

The fox turning back just look
irreducible mass is irreducible
this answer is independent of location.
The same & not the same a path of scatters.

Who lives there now? A character from an old book
could fall away & all there in momentary apex modernism
the relationship between exterior derivatives.
Did she follow the fox or the lightening says nothing.

Not fire but its deep blue core.
10 years ago, a complicated timepiece,
next a master clock
like writing by hand but nobody's hand no the hand of electricity.

0.0.2.1

Threads through scratches on this soft wood
this energy is being dissipated internally
living starlight paper geometry & secrets.
The soft comfort of small hunger

revising light fall freely & unconstrained.
This close to the end come back to it:
use these metric components & the components
forget. These aren't your memories anyway.

How it becomes cliché or stuck not dissolving,
buy old watches disassemble them & determine by practical observation
a thrush was singing but it's quiet now.
Canonical memories. More winter pages.

It's blown away & sure you could catch the torn page
cathedral window test-pattern colour chosen by chance.
So & always information, decay,
& either the well was very deep or the fall very slow, plenty of time—

0.0.2.2

Continuous action begun in the past & continuing,
falling & disappears in the dry cold air sublimation,
mathematical notation for events, coordinates & vectors.
If self falls apart in pebbles or bread crumbs—

The cat sleeping, dreaming under the desk lamp where it's warm.
Feather of breath on skin
the sun's glare on this page until I adjust the blinds.
Unrecognized names wasted teleology or a diary

emotion tangled up in cool not colour / scatter.
A few children wondering at the clotted clouds
midday, unopened books unfinished doubt.
Uncertain if there are figures without boundaries

another recollection or expectation questions
if it is a homeomorphism onto its image is
always in the present tense. No going back. The house anticipated at the end
of time & weather.

0.0.2.3

Canonical memories. More winter pages.
Stars perhaps small holes burnt through paper as children
energy quantum fluctuations of inertia
far from a stationary, fully relativistic source

not contradiction a salamander in the fire or at your feet at the threshold
which is different from the bees in the purple sage scent
propagation of gravitational waves.
Here at the table writing by hand & rewriting by memory a few phrases

there are too many sheets of paper not
the mark or ash or plumb line blue.
Inspiration. Shards of saints & stories blown apart—
she played, chalk on sidewalk, Himmel oder Hölle, Angry Birds—

love & strife or is it love & disease or theft & early transcendentals.
Balconies wooden stairs in the snow in another city still
what colour their ashes are & if digital ashes differ from analog.
No site or formal counterpoint no machine of time.

0.0.3.0

Set words down on the red chair at the top of the stairs
& these aren't my ruins to stumble over
more difficult than coming through nothing.
Breathless & hopeful unbroken distance. Forgetting & retelling.

The feel & smell of an old book not death held open in 2 hands
& for example on page 435 weak gravitational fields
continuous action begun in the past & continuing.
Read astronomy answer questions with evasion anything like truth.

Apples dried up into sketches
to come or being lived through.
At a certain time, time is inconsequential
obsolete beautiful loops & spirals of charge & condensation

uncertain if there are figures without boundaries
neither noise nor silence uncertain bright
dead raven & carrion bird in the grass. Flies.
One voice or many, one then many.

0.0.3.1

Read again. Nothing beautiful. Gardens
argument or conspiracy, perhaps endearments, seduction—
when I was just winter streets
infinite but another sense the wind takes them & the rain.

Mass of this invisible component
at this table scraps of the 20th century measured out
the typography of the past repeated.
After the above analysis of any one hypersurface of homogeneity

falling disappears in the dry cold air sublimation
of familiar lines recalled & copying them out
by hand the sky, now weather,
the equation of state used in constructing the equilibrium.

That time seems impossible, unrepeatable now.
Over years & so the rose garden & everybody knows the ruined chapels
      country houses broken cities
& these aren't my ruins to stumble over.
Unrecognized names wasted teleology or a diary.

0.0.3.2

The small change in flavour, a sharper maybe, iron.
Uncertain if there are figures without boundaries.
Reading it all again requires return
at least I'll fill this page. Always one more thing

slightly downhill sound a trowel spreading cement
& in the process disconnects its outer regions
no skill to put better words to those colours—
Desire or geometry is a conversation an orchestra

without memory rust or other words
quick corners in this cottage or gentrified row house
refusing motion & stillness at once all real places.
Even when names remain who is there to say

the trees filling in the light more patterned sidewalk & quiet I get distracted.
In unusual coordinates an artifact of viewpoint centrifugal
branches unrecognized decisions different lives.
Elliptical, allusive vague light.

0.0.3.3

A war. A shattered glass. Your eyes are still
the remainder
or leave pages blank nothing uncovered
not concerned not looking at old photographs or letters or emails

unrecognized names wasted teleology or a diary
branches unrecognized decisions different lives—
Always falling wind before the firestorms adding up histories.
Not wanting to answer this year's question

producing new vector fields from old.
Canonical memories. More winter pages.
Who lives there now? A character from an old book.
Directly informative, but to learn about the coordinates

if the vector field generates an isometry
is about to break the time.
Doesn't it drop away another red thread or prophecy another
thick paint, without a determined design, watching?

& if I interrupt myself again
& again
just loss itself. How loss is written
on the edge of everything, a library
arranged in order after
the fact. Fitting the facts,
predictive & sensible, that
there was a reason for all this, that—

& if I interrupt myself
for a third time
& there are 20 words missing
it doesn't
mean anything but that
doesn't mean it isn't
beautiful. Again:
is that—

9

0.1.0.0

I know still. Left of the day.

Desire or geometry is a conversation an orchestra

(mathematics was not sufficiently refined in 1917)

she played, chalk on sidewalk, Himmel oder Hölle, Angry Birds —

Time & weather

saturating everything that absence is unwritten on.

Now treat the static, spherically symmetric field as the field of the sun,

ask how long forgetting takes

throwing my keys off the bridge out onto the ice & walking away the
    damage

without need recurs & varies unconcerned

local Lorenz geometry & local Euclidean geometry

not about memory or every

child writing on a slate the book closed resting outside

some dream of history, dreams of almost

polygons & scattered tools / compass &

at liberty. Before decision. In contemplation.

0.1.0.1

New cathedral windows colour & colour
chance falling together
& apart of light. History scraped away.
Memory still rehearsed & mistaken

always walking a shattered road of
small packages & precious improvisations.
"All time is unredeemable" its order only
imposed by the desire for order another network

of branching light & dark displaced covariant derivatives
life burnt away radiant life & no ash of words
on broken glass gravestones, thorn bushes growing.
2:38 pm. Partly cloudy for the hour.

How often again looking at them & looking
at them while they step back
in the past as territories measure
shadows may not be leaves.

0.1.0.2

What grace this leaves us with to be
opened out & reread what value & answering
sky falling along every geodesic
not a long walk but wondering if it's going to rain.

2:47 pm. Overcast. The forecast doesn't call for it.
Some are detained at the border & will not pass.
Some dream of history, dreams of almost
forgotten anchorites, tungsten & unmaking—

Perhaps there are gaps.
To preserve, to elevate, to cancel.
No time to find out stopping
means more than already 8:06 pm.

"The inner freedom from practical desire"
having to live with these memories
black & white on playing cards metro tickets luscious Japanese paper
& either the well was very deep or the fall very slow, plenty of time—

0.1.0.3

"Turning shadow into transient beauty"
always beginning as ashes begin
as objects end as objects
& no different disperse now & eventually

small tonal transitions of the black & white past
in another city of grey stones somewhat abstract
sometimes melancholy lacking mirrors
without a theory of history, ruins, indifference—

11:04 am. Mostly cloudy. Light rain starting in 15 minutes
so nothing begins because the breath
is held, the body is held, tension in the calves & shoulders
no thought no thought no thought

no wristwatches stopped at random times
no brown paper & twine & wrapping paper
no photocopies of prints by Dürer vacation postcards or beach stones
no ticket stubs or pocket journal datebooks or cups full of coloured pencils
   & war poetry or volumes of the Stockholm edition of the works of
   Thomas Mann—

0.1.1.0

New cathedral windows colour & colour
chance falling together
& apart of light. History scraped away.
Memory still rehearsed & mistaken

unacknowledged experience unspoken for
resists narrative to leave breathing in & breathing out
3:50 pm sunset at 4:51 pm overcast for the next hour
& rain this evening full moon above the clouds.

It doesn't have to make sense like a welder
or Kensington or Copenhagen, encrypted dark
matter implied by its effect on observables
not the act itself or alone.

Perhaps forgetting is pure unknowing possible
"then a cloud passed & the pool was empty."
No depth, no shadows. Navigate
clock time in silence / no return / one way.

0.1.1.1

One seeks a solution that is continuous over the closed manifold &
   everywhere
become relativistically degenerate
in place of the "geometric" principle of extremal length
the first time to structure repetition. No one taught me that raised

what grace this leaves us with to be.
By hand, imperfect concentration but applying it directly,
time & weather
from memory not life / by heart —

knitted or knotted or woven with no pattern or vanishing —
action conditioned & dependent still life
matter implied by its effect on observables
or leave pages blank nothing uncovered

or even battalion records more than
may cause a change in structure
emptiness itself & wind & forgetting possibly
rose garden & fox & voices half heard or half understood —

0.1.1.2

12:08 pm. Overcast. Reliable quiet after rain
cool spring & a few early flowers
iris reticulata blue as the beginning
of night & yellow crocus uncomplicated

slow anniversaries marking the fixed frame
of life. Rewriting the same pages.
Not meaning but morning that fails
& fails again, no better for being / repeated

thinking they matter or they don't, taking refuge
in thoughts that are not treasures at all
repeating empty hands & an empty glass
where to end the line the stanza / page.

Forgetting now & totally attentive
to it or say so is this
self-deception modernism
"& is silent, the light is still."

0.1.1.3

When scattered or lost or noise or
falling turbulence not an atlas not
directions not a guide not definitive
not coherent except by accident

by geometry & the allegory of the Riemann curvature tensor
"caught in the form of limitation"
some left out after all those missing
some short lines or a poem

which isn't a story at all except when it is.
2:05 pm. Windy this evening, with snow throughout the day.
The crack in the glass is part of it & the shadow
left or etched or burnt by the air-burst in a different city

breathing porcelain & asbestos
wet iron water seeping below roots hiding
under roots rotting old growth
& too many paths to find a way.

0.1.2.0

Perhaps forgetting is pure unknowing possible
understanding something of it as it comes apart.
No depth, no shadows. Navigate
clock time in silence / no return / one way

by geometry & the allegory of the Riemann curvature tensor
an infinite number of solutions to these equations
some left out after all those missing
some short lines or a poem

"& the old made explicit, understood"
curving / falling / recited / absence
4:32 pm clear clear for the hour
lines crossed out

in rough outline arranged & unarranged / disarranged
here not present but present
this far away it's almost Euclidean
contradiction that is real feeling.

0.1.2.1

The difficulty of knowing data on the whole of a spacelike surface
not wanting to answer this year's question
& the possibility that even if one did it would still be insufficient.
10 years ago, a complicated timepiece.

Nevertheless despite these limitations one can still predict
today being today again, black, violet &
the occurrence of singularities under certain conditions.
What was the weather like, the crossing?

Displacement or caesura the streets all about
pavement, cobblestones & green trolley cars
no longer modern for example 2:36 pm overcast
paint on paint on paint becoming vertigo

broken sleet, uncertain & solitary & even that
"has answered light to light, & is silent, the light is still"
to be precise. Outlines can be enough
or haunting, nothing or everything / empty.

0.1.2.2

Long since rebuilt in the modern style
in the absence of a metric
directions not a guide not definitive
to be 3-dimensional in the Schwarzschild coordinate system.

Revision stalls & interwoven tangles
the set of all points which can be reached
or wheels a sort of useless machine counting cannot be a poem.
Language of forms

direct, simple, a gift after a lot of labour that time actually
anchoring quiet it's possible to touch.
Who would want to give this up?
No thought no thought no thought

under roots rotting old growth
some left out after all those missing.
Making any decisions & what we still call lamplight
outside accurately scattered the same way—

0.1.2.3

The beginning is delight again.
Joy of it endless, embodiment
pure & outside time, & the memory
of joy is not joy but can perhaps—

action conditioned & dependent still life
without need recurs & varies unconcerned
unreliable celebration a future almost reconciled
"in a dignified & commodious sacrament"

should be or is it will have been
another recollection or expectation questions
to come or being lived through
a chain of alternatives unchosen / losses

for example instead of a photograph
this melody (listen!) slowly & then again
or fast & then 1:35 pm. Snow. Snow for the hour.
Why is repetition necessary?

0.1.3.0

By geometry & the allegory of the Riemann curvature tensor
all in elegy preceded rewritten read
some left out after all those missing
some short lines or a poem

spatter, leopard, the starry sky or smallpox scar
& writing by hand living inside this
eating an apple 3:16 pm sunny
a roomful of light / a door.

Since the microwave radiation seems to be
all-pervasive, any past-directed timelike geodesic
must pass through optical depth
as before there can be no significant opacity back to

this happened then this happened.
The clock counting frame by frame
flattening event & memory, error
"with slow rotation suggesting permanence."

0.1.3.1

By hand, imperfect concentration but applying it directly,
thick paint, without a determined design watching
or listening the unthought knowing a tangle
of neurochemistry & intention, provisional solutions

paper blown across the tabletop or shadows
not about memory or every
yearning which is to say notebook being
tired of images only leaves you with

12:08 pm. Overcast. Reliable quiet after rain
cool spring & a few early flowers
iris reticulata blue as the beginning
of night & yellow crocus uncomplicated

"only in time; but that which is only living"
& you just can't get your hands on it.
A difference between a secret & an apple tree,
a love letter & bibliography, geometry, the fox at the roadside.

0.1.3.2

"In my beginning is my end. In succession"
an essay of shards & swerves, strange attractors
calculable if not predictable metaphor
therefore inadequate covenant of time.

Cold stars above empty fields. Thick stiff mud. Hoarfrost.
The future & the past all empty. Dry stalks of Queen Anne's lace.
It would have been a meadow after,
before the cold, the presocratic fragments.

Not ashes or briar or a definite edge
lost in detail which is a certain common grey exterior
oil paint meaning for example there aren't very many hardware stores.
3:09 pm. Overcast for the hour & snow until tomorrow morning.

Then it curves & falls back to absence
all the old thoughts or just a thread
caught on something like an improvisation
out of time the fabric of belief.

0.1.3.3

A song even if every note is melancholia or a number
to consider loss when there was nothing.
Place names without places. Unrecognized smiles.
Familiar lines recalled & copying them out.

What you want is explanation & at some time or point
Jerome at his translations, a drafty room in Nuremberg,
in another city of grey stones somewhat abstract
one-parameter family of geodesics

interrupted by hawk migration in cloudless sky the self presented here &
is impossible even the memory of prayer—
I think Tom just perhaps but that passes,
flew off silent in the cool of the morning now

can be most easily examined by constructing a manifold,
can't call you back breathless & hopeful unbroken
irreversible trajectory past & out falling further forward.
Sublime melancholy! Is that the remainder?

& if I interrupt myself
for a fourth time
is something you have
to hold on to, time
like the snow angled
from the north like
the rain angled from
the east, no memory
or need of memory
losing everything at once
beyond recollection—

& if I interrupt myself
for a fifth time
maybe it means nothing to you.
Or meant nothing.
(What is nothing?)
At this time I'm left with a lot of paper
& lists of words
still, often, realize, empty &c
& that's not quite the—

5

0.2.0.0

To say nothing, feel nothing, remember nothing, think
black & white on playing cards metro tickets luscious Japanese paper
& no different disperse now & eventually
theorems on singularities

at once without certainty leaving me
enough to establish it in the preferred coordinate system—
there are no flowers & there—
There is anger. There is a war. A tearing. A dislocation.

Not noise or a diamond cutting through
line by line or cell by cell knowing what you know.
Valid for any vibrating resonant detector whatsoever
always parallel.

Time. Weather.
Numbers. Arrival. A place. A real place. A site of thought.
The set of all points which can be reached.
Memory still rehearsed & mistaken.

0.2.0.1

Which is a question of distance or burial
2:16 pm. Overcast. Overcast for the hour
as a coordinate transformation of grief
the typography of the past repeated

"& the outer compulsion, yet surrounded"
even in the absence of zero time
when I was just winter streets
slush browngrey or cardboard.

By geometry & the allegory of the Riemann curvature tensor
all in elegy preceded rewritten read
some left out after all those missing
some short lines or a poem

early, waking before dawn, walking
wet streets after rain meeting no one
look in all the usual places, prose now,
the delusion of black & white.

0.2.0.2

Letters yet to be read or all burnt
in strange duty closing the door on ruins
of machinery again. 3:42 pm. Overcast. Identifying
Dürer's *Melencolia* with the angel of history

thinking they matter or they don't, taking refuge
in thoughts that are not treasures at all
repeating empty hands & an empty glass
where to end the line the stanza or page.

Reading it all again requires return
& these aren't my ruins to stumble over
unrecognized names wasted teleology or a diary
"the knowledge imposes a pattern, & falsifies"

continuous action begun in the past & continuing.
Unlike grief this repetition the decision to copy
these by hand having learnt to write with a fountain pen
read astronomy answer questions with evasion anything like truth.

0.2.0.3

Into stories when there are no stories
the story is not the life / remembered
joy not joyous recalled fire not burning
the story of fire or joy now 5:40 pm mostly cloudy

"& what you do not know is the only thing you know"
understanding something of it as it comes apart.
No depth, no shadows. Navigate
clock time in silence / no return / one way.

At some point you have to stop reading.
Something has broken something
is about to break the time
a fox at the roadside at sunset.

No more bright punctuation or shiny word-coins.
Small breakfasts, sometimes in the garden.
Call it a garden. Like the description of a flower
the description of a scent or taste or touch.

0.2.1.0

12:08 pm. Overcast. Reliable quiet after rain
cool spring & a few early flowers
iris reticulata blue as the beginning
of night & yellow crocus uncomplicated

present moment stretching if
there are no flowers & there
are not understandings that
faint edge memory just a few words

only now knowing insofar as it is possible
& perhaps in error & not empty not pure
sit & turn it over & over in your otherwise
empty hands never done with.

"Be remembered; involved with past & future"
always walking a shattered road of
small packages & precious improvisations
its order only imposed by the desire for order.

0.2.1.1

The gold nib of a fountain pen, ink-scaled.
A prescription for attaching some kind of boundary.
Read again. Nothing beautiful. Gardens.
Call it a garden. Like the description of a flower

uncertain if there are figures without boundaries
or prose. Redemption. War. Loss.
Walking in winter under Orion to buy books
dynamics & some of their ramifications

like time caught in the cloud chamber's physical trace.
No site or formal counterpoint no machine of time.
Verify the one & disprove the other.
Inarticulate now

in the absence of a metric
or look down at the froth & flow, imagine
growing up among foreigners our native
small tonal transitions of the black & white past—

0.2.1.2

As if you could choose to remember or forget
ask what has been left interruption
lovely lists of the names of flowers
"that we are sound, substantial flesh & blood —"

the rest is battered, solitary, uncertain
an essay of shards & swerves, strange attractors
calculable if not predictable metaphor
therefore inadequate covenant of time

broken afterwards shell pits filled with rain or groundwater
& a thin skim of ice under clear sky &
a few children wondering at the clotted clouds
of the Milky Way almost accustomed to it

all they'll say decades later beginning partway down
a lifetime & still walking 4:43 pm the weather
unrecalled green leaves maybe no coat yet
I see I forgot the apple also.

0.2.1.3

Between deaths & gestures objects as raw as prayer
is impossible even the memory of prayer
a skinny dog sleeping by the millstone & the workshop's tumble
measurement & perspective exception & rule I can't speak to.

Leaf green plates on the table left outside
"& found & lost again & again; & now under conditions"
foreshadowing line breaks recalling
pools of rain & mossy stones, colder, wetter days getting shorter

when what are ashes or remembered
timepieces stopped broken willow shadows
washed by rain 10:57 pm & turbulence all
or some of the intermittencies of now revised

it wasn't like that. Ever. Steel & copper
wreckage piled to make a mountain.
Forest growing up around the workshop.
Greyblue parallels edging light, incantation, weather.

0.2.2.0

"What was to be the value of the long looked forward to"
after the ordinary dinner (bread, wine, apples) a few
words some kind most disinterested the wind unquestioning
& a song even if every note is melancholia or a number

but oh! the slanting light & everything it connects anachronism.
More has been forgotten than a list, than a score.
Say what you see. That worked before. An hourglass.
Jerome at his translations, a drafty room in Nuremberg.

Taking as a text the Principle of Equivalence
gravitation, acceleration, gift & given, being given, initial state
usually spatially separated can time
be torn up if I interrupt myself 3:27 pm partly cloudy—

A path of scatters as before unplanned
always beginning as ashes begin
as objects end as objects
& no different disperse now & eventually.

0.2.2.1

Now leaves dry & about to having
long enough ago thin between brittle dust or air
timestrewn & nightrisked unwrapped knotted entire or measure
the story set aside for another jewel green evasion—

toward bright noise aphorism & error
or hold your instruments & look away
from geometry & falling or falling. Drawing.
Deliberating & there is no refusal. 2:03 pm. Light rain.

Canonical memories. More winter pages.
The soft comfort of small hunger
anchoring quiet it's possible to touch
loss everyday snow melting in your palm.

That this is also love. That a utility van
a yellow green ladder trade name Featherlite
racked on its roof is parked across the street. Two orange pylons.
"That we are sound, substantial flesh & blood."

0.2.2.2

An isolated system of stars & nebulae.
New cathedral windows colour & colour
linked tangent space at neighbouring points
thick paint, without a determined design watching

the question of burial remains & if elegy
at the trestle table beside the high windows the fox & the lion—
infinite but another sense the wind takes them & the rain
energy gained from gravity

only pure grey bones left unburied ash of stars just stars & all the dark
    between
only imagination & entirely present recall
a mirror you could step through broken glass—
The total mass-energy of an isolated star

as if action were enough. What do you do after that, & after after?
Under fading dust wrappers sky blue cloth fine with no markings
of joy is not joy but can perhaps
be a constant of order unity.

0.2.2.3

This has changed not vividly the all clear
moments close to touching hold without
grasping in devotion like the raven or kingfisher.
3:52 pm. Sunlight through leaves & shadows

like the river statistics like solutions to these equations
evolve even with many documents destroyed paper
unlike bones or metal insignia of rank
or even battalion records more than

revision stalls & interwoven tangles
like morning glories! that celestial blue! leaning
toward glorious luminary night & our early evening city
spread beneath us like a vast constellation —

It wasn't like that. Ever. Steel & copper
"older than the time of chronometers, older"
forest growing up around the workshop.
Greyblue parallels edging light, incantation, weather.

0.2.3.0

A workshop, but nothing is built there.
Rose tangles & thistle overgrown flagstone paths
forest hedges dry pools rank ponds &
the graffiti'd gazebo, charred stones plastic aluminum shattered glass

toward bright noise aphorism & error
or hold your instruments & look away
from geometry & falling or falling. Drawing.
Deliberating & there is no refusal. 2:03 pm. Light rain.

Unending, unpunctuated by any equilibrium
but not chaotic / rules but not
one set. The haze that passes for clear sky.
Easy brokenness & rage without regret.

"I said to my soul, be still, & let the dark come upon you,"
built a low wall between the house & the street under the pines
dividing the living from the dead, like snow.
Light rain stopping in 25 minutes.

0.2.3.1

To unsay or undo or to say or do again not
exactly not remembered even if remembered
this unopened book set aside & from memory
lines curving falling recited lines crossed out

"isolated, with no before & after"
at a certain time, time is inconsequential.
Sit here with a book. The wind breathes.
A small plane passes over. Perhaps the thrush again but that's not so.

This happened then this happened.
The clock counting frame by frame
flattening event & memory, error
for the first time without time

no specifics, avoidance, disavowal
a game of silence circling a dark centre
words instead of feeling or real thought
if self falls apart in pebbles or bread crumbs —

0.2.3.2

12:57 pm. Clear. Clear for the hour.
Quickly. Tell repeatedly nothing at all nothing
in this quiet room not shoreline no waves
breaking the empty street the window still closed.

Scraps. Incompletions. Endings without beginnings.
Colour words without colour. Numbers without counting.
Place names without places. Unrecognized smiles.
No stories. A first memory perhaps not possible.

"Trying to unweave, unwind, unravel"
to consider loss when there was nothing
where grief should have been indeterminate geometry
sharp edges, diffuse shadows, breathing

emptiness itself & wind & forgetting possibly
a distant siren fire trash collection
remembering ash cans made of metal
grey galvanized past ringing details—

0.2.3.3

Pick an event & a tangent vector.
No tongues of flame. A small envelope containing
these & most other instances of the propagation of light
can be most easily examined by constructing a manifold

slightly downhill sound a trowel spreading cement
stopped the instant it comes into existence.
Proof that zero is always & everywhere. That time
nongeometrically.

A war. A shattered glass. Your eyes are still —
to the mark chalk or ash or plumb line blue
a distant siren fire trash collection
the rewriting replacing hours & hands, some empty

it's hard to tell what's leaving.
Time & weather
now reduces to the calculation of connection one-forms.
Rose tangles & thistle overgrown flagstone paths.

& if I interrupt myself
for a sixth time
but these are not poems
you said a wind
of words from the past blowing
us into the now, new
angles all of us listening
who can hear dictionaries & encyclopedias:
all, complete, eternity—
be—

& if I interrupt myself
for a seventh time
on to absence
interrupted & broken but
hazy, voices in the fog
divorced from distance, short
lines like rain.
People with newspapers creased
over their heads in the downpour
on the bridge
in an old—

16

0.3.0.0

At your feet papers in the wind imagine one copy
when what are ashes or remembered
between deaths & gestures objects as raw as prayer.
Sublime melancholy! Is that the remainder?

Usually spatially separated can time,
pavement, cobblestones & green trolley cars
idealizing the moon & sun as point masses
what tradition remains to be unfolded & reread?

That matter there governs inertia here
a curve that is straight & uniformly parameterized
salamander quick in the flames the coals ash jewelled eyes—
it scampers off just grey enough

not order or intermittent emptiness beginning.
If this step is not straightforward
notice this picture could fit perfectly well into a book on X-rays &
    crystallography
in black ink borrowed authority to replace feeling.

0.3.0.1

1:06 pm wind & grey head down
I feel alone & too much I
walking in winter under Orion to buy books
lines numbered avenues not Cartesian mapped

at the desk & making order of it
line by line or cell by cell knowing what you know.
Numbers. Arrival. A place. A real place. A site of thought.
Someone else has said this better.

When scattered or lost or noise or
falling turbulence not an atlas not
directions not a guide not definitive
not coherent except by accident

beginning with a place or with the end not beginning
not order or intermittent emptiness beginning
"is the same, not in movement"
outside accurately scattered the same way—

0.3.0.2

Cloud of unknowing brief & always cloud
of forgetting that cloud shaped like
a continent a coastline foam left
by waves breaking before the next wave knowing

"something I have said before. I shall say it again."
Mechanical time. This then that. The stem
(like an apple) to set the time by reference
to another time or the sky / the escapement

of familiar lines recalled & copying them out
by hand (12:04 pm. Mostly cloudy for the hour.) the sky
could fall away & all there in momentary apex modernism
untainted anyway what could come after

paper blown across the tabletop or shadows
not about memory or every
yearning which is to say notebook being
tired of images only leaves you with —

0.3.0.3

Is it enough or more than enough
"while emotion takes to itself the emotionless"
small wind written by hand just disturbs
children watching airplanes dream.

Sublime melancholy! Is that the remainder?
A place in between where you wait without
making any decisions & what we still call lamplight
through uncertain windows even this comfort is no inside.

1:28 pm. Light snow for the hour & quiet
starlight falling into a well becoming violet with falling
snow fills the air this way then that way & the way
up is the way down always looks different.

Not even one cold full stop of feeling
only slant lines thin memory
& no shelter visible. Precise parallels in 2 directions
a mirror you could step through broken glass—

0.3.1.0

Raining again there are 2 rhythms
"time before & time after"
steady rain rainwater running off the roof
2 rhythms & neither regular

figurative realist narrative description
anyway looking at them
for hours the world almost
falling away. It never did.

Who would want to give this up?
The wind diaspora of answers geodesic
never void & always void
clocks fast / slow / in phase & slipping 2:48 am

the existence of an apparent horizon
implies a component of the event horizon
outside it or coinciding
the converse not necessarily.

0.3.1.1

I thought I saw something in your eyes
accumulation over years & unsymmetric silence:
the conviction that the necessity of our geometry cannot be demonstrated.
Self-deception modernism

oil paint meaning for example there aren't very many
descriptions in terms of curvature —
means more than already
less & less let's say the frame shrinks around the clock.

The vanishing of the divergence is not to be regarded as a consequence
untainted anyway what could come after
the Riemann matrix with vanishing Einstein tensor.
Emotion tangled up in cool not colour / scatter

through uncertain windows even this comfort is no inside.
There each event has its own tangent space
to break up the rhythm if this is a diary or worthless
the precarity of rubble without rhythm or self-similarity.

0.3.1.2

There are comets in our lifetime.
The speaking subject cannot be so easily
aureole, variable, wind again, warm skin.
Sound of the river below unseeded. Not winter.

Vicious slices & shards all edges
small sparks you keep finding for weeks
again & again every diamond cut into
sight. Like that. Or even a waterglass.

If you shatter into 1,000 (& one) stories
children playing in the street this afternoon
& singing (that's rare) in discordant concord
interrupted by reply & post arriving

predicted is that beautiful or ornament
"the murmuring shell of time, & not in any language"
proof that zero is always & everywhere that time
1:38 pm. Clear for the hour.

0.3.1.3

Perhaps there are gaps.
To preserve, to elevate, to cancel.
No time to find out stopping
means more than already 8:06 pm

sometimes a black white light radiance
saturating everything that absence is unwritten on
or does desire stream through & cannot be recalled
the noise of accidents

"setting forth & not returning"
resists narrative to leave breathing in & breathing out
3:50 pm sunset at 4:51 pm overcast for the next hour
& rain this evening full moon above the clouds

filling time with pages instead
of saying or doing / nothing left
uncertain if there are figures without boundaries
or coloured in bright tropic orange green or dark blue—

0.3.2.0

Cold rain too the bare tree on Crawford Street
clearly visible fractal reach of its branches
as if the purpose of light in another city to
glimpse a fox in this civil twilight London say—

All is not lost. To wonder what grace this leaves us with
what tradition remains to be unfolded & reread
what value & answering the sleepers in the underground
blacked-out windows & the few walking dark streets

alone. Without remembering or acting on memory.
"Something I have said before. I shall say it again."
At liberty. Before decision. In contemplation.
A pebble gathering speed only now again. 12:56 pm. Overcast

& this is the centre of the century the pane of glass the rock
hurled at the lightning cracks radiating before the slivers crash
silence not ending it still & fire not ending it & ashes not ending it
every language burnt & written on air hot metal & dust—

0.3.2.1

To unsay or undo or to say or do again not
exactly not remembered even if remembered
this unopened book set aside & from memory
lines curving falling recited lines crossed out

slow anniversaries mark the fixed frame
"of wistful regret for those who are not yet here to regret."
Not meaning but morning that fails
& fails again, no better for being / repeated.

There may be better things to do.
Walk in the cold clear air & not
wear a watch or think about the time
what to do later today or tomorrow.

3:08 pm. Partly cloudy. Partly cloudy for the hour.
There are some true things or things thought to be true
& so shrines are built outside cause & effect.
It's all there. A hologram. Vulture Peak or the Paradiso.

0.3.2.2

The child neglected in overwhelming
we did that magnifying glass well mainly the corners
say each independent & whole
a circle of folded slices of the night sky.

Something has broken something.
It felt good to close the door.
Joy of it endless, embodiment
describes infall through the horizon in a faithful, non-singular way

to unsay or undo or to say or do again not
a workshop, but nothing is built there
knitted or knotted or woven with no pattern or vanishing
without edges & everything inside time & weather.

Or look down at the froth & flow, imagine
everything I do not have & cannot —
night & yellow crocus uncomplicated
accusation innocence & guilt unknowing as displaced —

0.3.2.3

It felt good to close the door
safe as houses
let daily life get on without looking.
"For most of us, there is only the unattended"

early, waking before dawn, walking
wet streets after rain meeting no one
look in all the usual places, prose now,
the delusion of black & white.

1:28 pm. Light snow for the hour & quiet
starlight falling into a well becoming violet with falling
snow fills the air this way then that way & the way
up is the way down always looks different.

The question of burial remains & if elegy
or something black can't say another word
but always another's words the beautiful
or the fox unexpected & subtle.

0.3.3.0

Unreliable time in a froth of emptiness
& what could be known raw material
of an abandoned avenue
long since rebuilt in the modern style

"or the sudden fury, is what it always was"
sans brilliant vision in sunlight 11:46 am
without skill or apology the wind & building breathing
fragments & suspicion sometimes an insincere act—

Red thread ties the hours not
a fabric or a net not that
regular looking back to see
causes or the singularity of forgetting

that time clear-eyed & immaculate
as yet the question how much is lost
not yet & then after there is a word
that time is not temporal—

0.3.3.1

Not even one cold full stop of feeling
only slant lines thin memory
& no shelter visible. Precise parallels in 2 directions
a mirror you could step through broken glass —

an action continuing in the present
that continuity the assumption taking up past
& future memory rewritten but not all
the rewriting replacing hours & hands, some empty

"setting forth & not returning"
to the mark chalk or ash or plumb line blue
& after that what does zero mean.
Sky the colour of that mark. The new world.

12:39 pm. Mostly cloudy. Mostly cloudy for the hour.
Devote yourself to calculation, enumeration
not the same as memory or a book or a wristwatch.
There are still a few pages left.

0.3.3.2

11:04 am. Mostly cloudy. Light rain starting in 15 minutes
so nothing begins because the breath
is held, the body is held, tension in the calves & shoulders
no thought no thought no thought

to consider loss when there was nothing
"the point of intersection with the timeless"
where grief should have been indeterminate geometry
sharp edges, diffuse shadows, breathing

a circle of folded slices of the night sky
in someone else's hand of questions
free of the past in the present repeatedly
6:01 pm. Partly cloudy. Partly cloudy for the hour.

The rest is battered, solitary, uncertain
an essay of shards & swerves, strange attractors
calculable if not predictable metaphor
therefore inadequate covenant of time—

0.3.3.3

Every language burnt & written on air hot metal & dust
regular solids, cone, polyhedron, calendar & timepiece.
Every shard its own trajectory, beyond ballistic falling free
& it was autumn & there was a kingfisher—

Or say so is this
how the words differ when interrupted is memory / is time
wet streets after rain meeting no one—
Breathless & hopeful unbroken distance. Forgetting & retelling.

Action completed in the past or action
of the broken glass at the roadside
only pure grey bones left unburied ash of stars just stars & all the dark
    between
pictorial representation in absence of a metric.

Craters merging on the coast of ruins the rain pooling there
redshift continued in anisotropic cosmology
to another time or the sky / the escapement
not coherent except by accident.

& if I interrupt myself
for an eighth time
words & deaths & words intertwine.
Scattered like sand, art. No, more.
Our times lacking ritual & the tragedy
we pretend otherwise. Out of these
splinters raise
a window, random pain
& shattered light shredded paper
as if—

& if I interrupt myself
for a ninth time
inevitably, pictorially
asking if this
descriptive or prescriptive purity presents
the skein followed
back to an early evening,
park bench, trees, towers
of the city across the former
ravine not quite filled in
a—

15

1.0.0.0

Salamander quick in the flames the coals ash jewelled eyes—
the initial singularity
& the sun's glare on this page until I adjust the blinds.
Some darker clouds, time & weather,

the effect of tidal forces on
repetition is interruption sometimes avalanche.
How the words differ when interrupted is memory / is time
cold rain too the bare tree on Crawford Street

for hours the world almost
without a theory of history, ruins, indifference—
no one following memory rewritten pools at the curb where there
   should be reflections
usually spatially separated. Can time

mark chalk or ash or plumb line blue
radius much less than wavelength.
To unsay or undo or to say or do again not
difficult to touch this exactly being erased—

1.0.0.1

Another city in which strangers throng & buy
& rust painted over dull grey hulls or remembered
balconies wooden stairs in the snow in another city still
early winters almost remembered not exactly

for example instead of a photograph
this melody (listen!) slowly & then again
or fast & then 1:35 pm. Snow. Snow for the hour.
Why is repetition necessary?

That would say each independent & whole
contains reflects echoes &c all
with an undertone of ecstatic grammar.
Repeated small pieces even if self-correcting—

Vicious slices & shards all edges
small sparks you keep finding for weeks
"point to one end, which is always present"
sight. Like that. Or even a waterglass.

1.0.0.2

There's nothing special about these words.
Machine. Sparrow. Geodesic. Memory
of the precise colour of time deeper
rose blood rust heat eventually unreadable —

No more bright punctuation or shiny word-coins.
Small breakfasts, sometimes in the garden.
Call it a garden. Like the description of a flower
the description of a scent or taste or touch.

Irregular, small enough to hold & polished
so you can see yourself in its pitted facets.
4:16 pm. Mostly cloudy. For the hour.
In the shape of grief not even prose.

"The resolution of its partial horror"
fire without light or heat dark & pure burning.
The book will sag & melt, a dull pool & no stars.
Unrecalled therefore unrepeated. Unnumbered. One one one.

1.0.0.3

Missing rhythm of absence or silence punctuated vacuum
energy quantum fluctuations of inertia perhaps
how thought comes into mind or memory & arcs out
desire exploding that calm symmetry massing is it regret—

Turn the page. Memory is fire in its cabinet
fire without light or heat dark & pure burning.
The book will sag & melt, a dull pool & no stars.
Unrecalled therefore unrepeated. Unnumbered. One one one.

12:34 pm. Clear. Clear for the hour.
That time seems impossible, unrepeatable now.
Freedom or loss? Without edges or scatters.
The explanatory entropy on the wall

if I rewrote from memory & forgetting
"this is the one way & the other"
beginning with unrecognized constellations
salamander quick in the flames the coals ash jewelled eyes—

1.0.1.0

Sans brilliant vision in sunlight morning
without skill or apology the wind & building breathing
"had the look of flowers that are looked at"
fragments & suspicion sometimes an insincere act

like the river statistics like solutions to these equations
evolve even with many documents destroyed paper
unlike bones or metal insignia of rank
or even battalion records more than

I stopped listening
built a low wall between the house & the street under the pines
dividing the living from the dead, like snow.
Light rain stopping in 25 minutes.

7:23 pm. By heart or memory not belief
in this place in this time maybe only
nostalgia is possible that pain
all that's left of homecoming now.

1.0.1.1

Turn the page. Memory is fire in its cabinet,
not a new idea ongoing like rain or time
fire only breathes in & ascends. Chemical fire.
A yellow green ladder trade name Featherlite

figurative realist narrative description
& what could be known raw material.
Knowing the components of the gradient one can calculate the
     components
of a field or a handful & in time falling far enough

is a convenient name for the vector.
Life burnt away radiant life & no ash of words
a source that is arbitrarily stressed & has arbitrary—
so nothing begins because the breath

fire without light or heat dark & pure burning
the scratching on the paper empty which is different than erased.
To keep a record & this is not a record
timepieces stopped broken willow shadows—

1.0.1.2

Apples dried up into sketches
"answered light to light, & is silent, the light is still"
leafing out into unrecognized constellations branching
geodesics that could have been or will have been if 1:38 pm. Partly cloudy.

Now leaves dry & about to having
long enough ago thin between brittle dust or air
timestrewn & nightrisked unwrapped knotted entire or measure
the story set aside for another jewel green evasion

no path retraced eyes closed wanting not
to listen to have
without memory rust or other words
from memory not life / by heart—

Read again. Nothing beautiful. Gardens
or the wildness of gardens as recalled
looking closely at the curl of small dimensions
oath of stones & maple keys / bicycle bells / collapse—

1.0.1.3

Set words down on the red chair at the top of the stairs
never & always only geometry not at a distance
the sun's glare on this page until I adjust the blinds
revising light fall freely & unconstrained

where you can stand in the middle
"under the tension, slip, slide, perish"
or look down at the froth & flow, imagine
writing water & rocks, not even that in winter.

No more bright punctuation or shiny word-coins.
Small breakfasts, sometimes in the garden.
Call it a garden. Like the description of a flower
the description of a scent or taste or touch.

Into stories when there are no stories
the story is not the life / remembered
joy not joyous recalled fire not burning
the story of fire or joy now 5:40 pm mostly cloudy.

1.0.2.0

Not a new idea ongoing like rain 5:28 pm
unremembered the detail edge past cutting
a photograph I didn't take of my mother as a girl in winter
to break up the rhythm if this is a diary or worthless

always walking a shattered road of
small packages & precious improvisations
its order only
imposed by the desire for order another network

annunciation of nothing by nothing still
rose garden & fox & voices half heard or half understood
children's voices because they were children
& it was autumn & there was a kingfisher —

Taking as a text the Principle of Equivalence
gravitation, acceleration, gift & given, being given, initial state
usually spatially separated can time
"& the old made explicit, understood —"

1.0.2.1

To consider loss when there was nothing
where grief should have been indeterminate geometry
sharp edges, diffuse shadows, breathing
thin memory if I interrupt myself

growing up among foreigners our native
speech an imposter unmarked by signs
watching closely what's expected & only once asking
what you knew. 10:23 pm. Clear for the hour.

Slow anniversaries mark the fixed frame
of life. Rewriting the same pages
"has answered light to light, & is silent, the light is still"
& fails again, no better for being / repeated.

Make a space becoming invisible
in a rush for it to be over & then, now
will have a shape. Polyhedron.
A book beginning this & ending time, or burnt & one.

1.0.2.2

Letters yet to be read or all burnt
real & all of it properly radiant life / beautiful desire / gift
(experimental tests of general relativity)
& no different disperse now & eventually

the same & not the same a path of scatters—
having lost my way in connections but not connected
the occurrence of singularities under certain conditions.
I wrote letters that were answered

the set of all points which can be reached
& rust painted over dull grey hulls or remembered
at that beginning even if the fox knows gnawing on silences
to presuppose existence & uniqueness.

Unlike grief this repetition the decision to copy
it's small & always far away. That war ended 70 years ago. That war.
The broken glass at the roadside.
All shall be well enough not that I believe any such thing only.

1.0.2.3

If the form will carry through
deep sapphire in a book.
Not fire but its deep blue core.
"If you do not come too close, if you do not come too close —"

Vicious slices & shards all edges
small sparks you keep finding for weeks
again & again every diamond cut into
sight. Like that. Or even a waterglass.

Impossible to see time.
11:05 am. Light snow for the hour.
Only trees threading light netted by the wind.
What wasn't found.

No wristwatches stopped at random times
no brown paper & twine & wrapping paper
no photocopies of prints by Dürer vacation postcards or beach stones
no ticket stubs or pocket journal datebooks or cups full of coloured pencils
   & war poetry or volumes of the Stockholm edition of the works of
   Thomas Mann.

1.0.3.0

1:06 pm wind & grey head down
"investing form with lucid stillness"
walking in winter under Orion to buy books
lines numbered avenues not Cartesian mapped

breathing porcelain & asbestos
wet iron water seeping below roots hiding
under roots rotting old growth
& too many paths to find a way.

The beginning is delight again.
Joy of it endless, embodiment
pure & outside time, & the memory
of joy is not joy but can perhaps

ask how long forgetting takes.
Desire or geometry is a conversation an orchestra
without recollection in the time it takes to read this.
The book should not have page numbers.

1.0.3.1

The precarity of rubble without rhythm or self-similarity.
Places in the forest where bones surface 50 years after
the crime. Not here. Maybe a zipper pull. A rivet.
The gold nib of a fountain pen, ink-scaled.

There is no plan, just repetition. Another page.
3:10 pm. Overcast for the hour.
Any beginning breaks the smooth surface &
recollection returns, breathing becomes difficult again, wearying

sans brilliant vision in sunlight
"not that only, but the co-existence"
without skill or apology the wind & building breathing
fragments & suspicion sometimes an insincere act.

Water over rocks & what's left of the mill a constant distribution
of frequencies of froth & foam the result of runoff from farm fields
stocked brown trout leaping parabolic geodesics remember
a catenary arc is not a parabola it's weighted down.

1.0.3.2

2:12 pm. Clear. Clear for the hour. The time before.
Fire only breathes in & ascends. Chemical fire.
Not an element. Every differentiable symmetry
of the action has a corresponding conservation law.

Geometry & after pale light misinterpreted
a cloud of unknowing again
seed pods blown, dried after one winter,
"across the open field, leaving the deep lane."

No question of flame or purity, refined
inarticulate now
is prose isn't it? Sometimes
it's hard to tell what's leaving.

It wasn't like that. Ever. Steel & copper
wreckage piled up to make a mountain.
Forest growing up around the workshop.
Greyblue parallels edging light, incantation, weather.

1.0.3.3

Of certain simple tensors in the context of a local Lorentz frame
deep sapphire in a book
or haunting, nothing or everything / empty.
Of some significance like a wheelbarrow or the internet hold it in your

fall toward a Schwarzschild black hole
continuing in the present life.
No abandoned country churches, worn-away gravestones, overgrown
    rosebushes,
old loves & current to address, letters, on paper

in rough outline arranged & unarranged / disarranged.
The unkempt awkward folding flap of wings after they land
light as fast as possible the ruin of time,
of history there alone & in company, in place

& a thin skim of ice under clear sky &
quick motion all corners in this cottage or gentrified row house.
Void scattered & complex
by determining the time delay.

& if I interrupt myself
for a tenth time
the way you all must have walked halfway
across Europe in the dark
in the cold away along broken
roads almost
alone. Diaspora never regathered.
Worn-out decades you walked
toward, & yes
you are—

& if I interrupt myself
for an eleventh time
all this time all
these frozen years & liquid
attempts to feel & think
it through despair
at everything undone
every letter unwritten meeting
missed all
our tools scattered
words scattered only
other people's books
I—

6

1.1.0.0

Many repetitions / highest apple / tree or fox—
at the desk & making order of it.
It wasn't like that. Ever. Steel & copper
limits on the usefulness of the concept of cross-section.

Displacement or caesura the streets all about
the only tensor constructible from & linear in second derivatives of metric
deficit, neglect. An unidentified rage & a closed door, a locked door,
a cloud of unknowing again

between the sun's acceleration of aluminum & gold
& writing by hand living inside this.
Pour paint on all those pages. Go for a walk around the block.
The occurrence of singularities under certain conditions

slightly different & a small change in flavour
used to measure spacetime intervals
calculation of the moment of rotation.
How can one write down the laws?

1.1.0.1

Like the river statistics like solutions to these equations
starting to the rain slowing back to polyrhythm
time. Without philosophy, occupation, charge, beyond
fixed uniquely by momentum.

Inarticulate now
sometimes melancholy lacking mirrors
& rain this evening full moon above the clouds.
Elliptical, allusive vague light.

What tradition remains to be unfolded & reread
imagining apple tree branches bare the same way the same network not
the child neglected in overwhelming.
The question of burial remains & if elegy

is slightly downhill sound a trowel spreading cement
perspectives on curvature
sum of the kinetic energy & gravitational potential energy is
an idealized collapsing star.

1.1.0.2

Different from the moment you're certain you're out of the woods
    across the frontier all clear
it's all there. A hologram. Vulture Peak or the Paradiso
& it was autumn & there was a kingfisher—
mathematics was not sufficiently refined in 1917.

Mass-energy inside radius r
without recollection in the time it takes to read this.
The smell of death unforgettable revolting sweetness
never & always only geometry not at a distance—

That this is also love. That a utility van,
a positive constant of order unity given by
obsolete beautiful loops & spirals of charge & condensation
missing rhythm of absence or silence punctuated vacuum,

not ashes or briar or a definite edge
directly informative, but to learn about the coordinates
the materials enough in themselves
no matter how beautiful go looking for shadows.

1.1.0.3

Without wires gears ailerons condensers just grey & some vibration
a place we can walk through a house or a neighbourhood —
only imagination & entirely present recall
if you are real or the children's voices

infinite but another sense the wind takes them & the rain.
What to do later today or tomorrow?
Places in the forest where bones surface 50 years after
contain reflect echo &c all —

Far-off construction. A power saw.
Machine. Sparrow. Geodesic. Memory.
Inspiration. Shards of saints & stories blown apart —
long enough ago thin between brittle dust or air

when what are ashes or remembered
in a rush for it to be over & then, now,
the crime. Not here. Maybe a zipper pull. A rivet.
A drawerful of stainless-steel cubes some with fine threaded holes.

1.1.1.0

Unrecognized names wasted teleology or a diary.
All this, every object, field, connection to a past reaching out to
    futures all the sinews between them bunched here—obviously / stop.
Change in a field relative to the parallel
aberration, incoming photon

but time has no scent no trace is framed by memory.
Unending, unpunctuated by any equilibrium
mathematical notation for events, coordinates & vectors
in rough outline arranged & unarranged / disarranged

moments close to touching hold without—
because there's no end to it & is that supposed to be a comfort?
Or the fox unexpected & subtle.
There are no flowers & there,

thought, intent, grace, silence, mind, truth,
sharp edges, diffuse shadows, breathing
neither noise nor silence uncertain bright
rose blood rust heat eventually unreadable—

1.1.1.1

Snow fills the air this way then that way & the way
pictorial representation in absence of a metric
self-deception, modernism
for example the difficulty deducing the metric tensor from measurements

walking in winter under Orion to buy books.
Not ashes or briar or a definite edge
or some of the intermittencies of now revised
what value & answering the sleepers in the underground

no thought no thought no thought.
No beginning is the highest truth I've heard.
Desire exploding that calm symmetry massing is it regret—
Time. Weather. A key turning. Plain text. A door.

The same again, don't remember
it or say so is this
let daily life get on without looking.
Raining again there are 2 rhythms.

                             & if I interrupt myself
again or for the twelfth time
leaving us then at the right time perhaps
but who's to judge but you
to tangle all those or these times
we tried
maybe we tried & made
time for a while from the tangles—

1.1.1.2

Uncertain if there are figures without boundaries
nothing up my sleeve. Except now a lion,
that voice these voices & how that implicates not enough to
  continue—
thick paint, without a determined design watching

what tradition remains to be unfolded & reread.
Hold fast. Time. Weather
under fading dust wrappers sky blue cloth fine with no markings or
  annotations to return to
the ashes of stories memories of fire & the sound of fire

undone unlived self shattering into myriad
I think Tom just perhaps but that passes.
For example instead of a photograph
the wave function collapses again & again in melancholy geometry.

The crack in the glass is part of it & the shadow
flattening event & memory, error
unlike grief this repetition the decision to copy
neither a philosopher nor a war—

1.1.1.3

As if you could choose to remember or forget
lines curving falling recited lines crossed out
walls & bridges, heights & ruins or else choice redeemed.
Living starlight paper geometry & secrets

understanding something of it as it comes apart
imposed by the desire for order. Another network
Dürer's *Melencolia* or the angel of history.
That this is also love. That a utility van

local Lorenz geometry & local Euclidean geometry
pour paint on all those pages. Go for a walk, around the block
convenient forgetting & unasked for
the lane warm lit windows in the twilight woods torn clouds thin moon.

I see I forgot the apple also.
In a rush for it to be over & then, now
proof that zero is always & everywhere that time
joy of it endless, embodiment.

1.1.2.0

An immersion is said to be an imbedding.
Because of its generality, this theorem does not tell us,
saturating everything that absence is unwritten on,
time conjectured, unremembered, walking

measures something. Quickly. Again. Quickly.
A list of is that beautiful or symbolic the rose garden voices of
revision interrupt myself with memory.
How much hope doesn't matter. A crystal palace collapsing

different from the moment you're certain you're out of the woods
    across the frontier all clear.
Remember. A small dog barking at the garbage collectors,
that the light cone is tangent to the horizon.
Place names without places. Unrecognized smiles.

The sound of an airliner climbing over the wind
here alone those moments it curls up tight coherent causal.
Not there can't vanish it does,
into stories when there are no stories—

1.1.2.1

Never & always only geometry not at a distance
by waves breaking before the next wave knowing
along integral curves from a given point
but oh! the slanting light & everything it connects anachronism.

Equation of state
of the broken glass at the roadside
used to measure spacetime intervals.
Scraps. Incompletions. Endings without beginnings.

Returning without memory this last time again
(like an apple) to set the time by reference.
One seeks a solution that is continuous over the closed manifold &
    everywhere
a deficit. A neglect. An unidentified rage & a closed door, a locked door.

Timestrewn & nightrisked unwrapped knotted entire or measure
some of the geometrical properties of a manifold
make a space becoming invisible.
The cat sleeping on the piano again. Sun through the blinds.

1.1.2.2

Why is repetition necessary?
Only pure grey bones left unburied ash of stars just stars & all the
    dark between
some short lines or a poem
three-dimensional in the Schwarzschild coordinate system

the vanishing of the divergence is not to be regarded as a consequence.
Sound of the river below unseeded. Not winter.
Cities of rooftops & streets bare trees against the lovely blueness of
    twilight.
After a fall, & in order: a landscape, a ghost, a reflection,

in black ink borrowed authority to replace feeling with—
only slant lines thin memory
encrypts itself & the key is lost
the child neglected in overwhelming

all-pervasive, any past-directed timelike geodesic
to read astronomy answer questions with evasion anything like truth.
Parallel transport to covariant derivative to geodesic.
Steady rain rainwater running off the roof.

1.1.2.3

Proof that zero is always & everywhere that time
whether the singularity will be in our past or in the future of our past.
Since the microwave radiation seems to be
refusal & execution

at the desk & making order of it
into radiant pixels worthless like life also unfinished
a story we could make up
& apart of light. History scraped away.

Sight. Like that. Or even waterglass
must pass through optical depth
tense experienced not reasoned intuition that
if it is a homeomorphism onto its image

which is different from the bees in the purple sage scent.
Watch each thought's trajectory through time as memory ravels
    round itself.
Again. Time. Weather. Every equation an approximation,
sharp edges, diffuse shadows, breathing.

1.1.3.0

As if you could choose to remember or forget
like time caught in the cloud chamber's physical trace
lines curving falling recited lines crossed out
the passage work & so much left

alone. Without remembering or acting on memory
like the river statistics like solutions to these equations
irreversible trajectory past & out falling further forward
temporal order & forgetting or disorder & error

exactly not remembered even if remembered
& writing by hand living inside this
so the submanifold may not intersect itself
because there's no end to it & is that supposed to be a comfort?

So & always information, decay.
A distant siren fire trash collection
breathing porcelain & asbestos
tinnitus of the quantum vacuum massed choir—

1.1.3.1

As if the purpose of light in another city
to preserve, to elevate, to cancel
moments close to touching hold without
freedom or loss. Without edges or scatters

at once without certainty leaving me.
The effect of tidal forces
but oh! the slanting light & everything it connects anachronism
& this is a world of shards & stories

small sparks you keep finding for weeks.
If the form will carry through
glimpse a fox in this civil twilight London say—
Inspiration. Shards of saints & stories blown apart,

Dürer's *Melencolia* with the angel of history
timestrewn & nightrisked unwrapped knotted entire or
peacetime measured out into this revised future square of numbers.
Light falls in these fields. Grain & furrows.

1.1.3.2

Contains reflects echoes &c all
reminding myself that I can delete this rewrite substantially—
out of time the fabric of belief.
The rewriting replacing hours & hands, some empty.

Raining again there are 2 rhythms.
There is no plan, just repetition. Another page.
Another time or the sky / the escapement
not meaning but morning that fails

continuing in the present life
& apart of light. History scraped away.
Technique of index gymnastics.
Cathedral window test pattern colour chosen by chance

by a library of wolves fresh cave fox shadows—
the smell of death unforgettable revolting sweetness.
Wear a watch or think about the time
to be precise. Outlines can be enough.

1.1.3.3

At this table scraps of the 20th century measured out.
The problem that words mean something
alone. Without remembering or acting on memory
or representation of a direction in space one of the stars in Orion,
    regarded—

Cross that out, it's gone now.
A net of geodesics not causation self-similarity
in the diagonal rain perhaps a stranger.
No wristwatches stopped at random times

tracing out the course of null geodesics.
Action completed in the past or action
no path retraced eyes closed wanting not—
Sky the colour of that mark. The new world.

Flattening event & memory, error.
Refusal & execution.
No prediction of spacetime, therefore no meaning for spacetime
if I rewrote from memory & forgetting—

& if I interrupt myself
again or for the thirteenth time
more than the continuation or
is it easy to ignore time's
signature—is that it?
For the time being
let me sign this
circle an empty
circle or broken
circle approximation
& hesitation
incompletion
the—

& if I interrupt myself
again or for the fourteenth time
which poem is that? Not mine, none of yours.
Martyrs & new martyrs maybe
but this isn't martyrdom these words
faithless. The fox, again. We disagreed. In time
we disagreed further, or more.
We didn't—

10

1.2.0.0

Not devotion or confession & without the force of ruins only numbers
yearning which is to say notebook being
of the action has a corresponding conservation law.
In the shape of grief not even prose.

In more than one book not to be reconciled the book closed.
Sublime melancholy! Is that the remainder?
Every shard its own trajectory, beyond ballistic falling free
a continent a coastline foam left—

Some truth in painting.
Cloud of unknowing brief & always cloud
wreckage piled up to make a mountain
with the measured annual variations of

imagined light tracking abstract across white walls.
Unrecalled therefore unrepeated. Unnumbered. One one one.
In special cases the story is almost as simple in 4 dimensions
all they'll say decades later beginning partway down.

1.2.0.1

I would like a chalkboard to write on to erase time & again
after strife or love swerve to silence
"has answered light to light & is silent, the light is still"
how to empty out the teaching.

Water over rocks & what's left of the mill a constant distribution
of frequencies of froth & foam the result of runoff from farm fields
stocked brown trout leaping parabolic geodesics remember
a catenary arc is not a parabola it's weighted down.

Spatter, leopard, the starry sky or smallpox scar
& writing by hand living inside this
eating an apple 3:16 pm sunny
a roomful of light / a door

left over after the fall & light in the windows
brittle sky. As if only in books. Just starting.
I know still. Left of the day.
4:23 pm. Partly cloudy for the hour.

1.2.0.2

Emptiness itself & wind & forgetting possibly
a distant siren fire trash collection
remembering ash cans made of metal &
"that we are sound, substantial, made of flesh & blood"

but there's no anger because anger is death that's right
there's no anger because why is there no.
There is anger. There is a war. A tearing. A dislocation.
Moonlight on blackout streets. Bodies & body parts. Erased.

Accusation innocence & guilt unknowing as displaced
children writing on a slate the book closed resting outside
regular solids, cone, polyhedron, calendar & timepiece
peacetime measured out into this revised future square of numbers

at once without certainty leaving me
to watch myself negotiate all that self—
Read this now. That word. Zero. What do you think?
4:23 pm. Partly cloudy.

1.2.0.3

In revision interrupt myself with memory.
War is not coincidence so.
Not chronologically ordered, not altered by the passage
only see it & only at times / darkly

spatter, leopard, the starry sky or smallpox scar
"or whatever event, this is your real destination"
eating an apple 3:16 pm sunny
a roomful of light / a door

left over after the fall & light in the windows
brittle sky. As if only in books. Just starting.
I know still. Left of the day.
4:23 pm. Partly cloudy for the hour.

Without a picture new names slipping
only tall & east & raven & field grey uncertain fog
unknowing as children as displaced
children home is where the —

1.2.1.0

Doesn't it drop away another red thread or prophecy another
list of is that beautiful or symbolic the rose garden voices of
how it becomes cliché or stuck not dissolving
into radiant pixels worthless like life also unfinished

accusation innocence & guilt unknowing as displaced
children writing on a slate the book closed resting outside
regular solids, cone, polyhedron, calendar & timepiece
peacetime measured out into this revised future square of numbers

marking time precisely or rough as sandpaper to smooth
branches unrecognized decisions different lives
the ashes of stories memories of fire & the sound of fire
"has answered light to light & is silent, the light is still"

the image of the past decaying into noise time being
distance scattering error quantum error & so
memory encrypts itself & the key is lost I never
or the markers of immediate sensation —

1.2.1.1

That time cannot be applied to them—
the trajectory & distribution having no unique source tree
the effect of tidal forces on
this room depending how you got here & where you started when

but not chaotic / rules but not
this far away it's almost Euclidean
so nothing begins because the breath
salamander quick in the flames the coals ash jewelled eyes—

Some dream of history, dreams of almost
"finite proper time," then, need not imply that any finite sequence of events
    was possible
coastline doubling back to television snow Orion.
Easy brokenness & rage without regret.

Theorems on singularities
colour words without colour. Numbers without counting
only begin & begin again & what's left after
tired of images only leaves you with—

1.2.1.2

Complex hierarchies fall away jewel by jewel
"taking the route you would be likely to take"
thought, intent, grace, silence, mind, truth
dispossessed, abstract & unbodied the way mathematics is

sometimes a black white light radiance
saturating everything that absence is unwritten on
or does desire stream through & cannot be recalled
the noise of accidents—

action conditioned & dependent still life
without need recurs & varies unconcerned
unreliable celebration a future almost reconciled.
5:05 pm. Windy this evening with snow throughout the day tomorrow.

No tongues of flame. A small envelope containing
a single sheet, some red thread untangled unknotted not yet stitched.
The first street lights & stars almost purple sky.
To the mailbox at the end of the block. Gone. Walk home.

1.2.1.3

In the diagonal rain perhaps a stranger
a slash of red at the cuff of a black sleeve the street
starting to the rain slowing back to polyrhythms
no one following memory rewritten pools at the curb where there
    should be reflections—

Time falls away or falls anyway geodesic
neither existent nor non-existent what is unknown
details leaving a general melancholia like sunlight
or prose. Redemption. War. Loss.

How often again looking at them & looking
at them while they step back
"while the dead leaves rattled on like tin"
shadows may not be leaves

rewritten from memory beginning the apple tree the tree
on Crawford I see from my window writing is a maple of course
imagining apple tree branches bare the same way the same network not
the same shape but similar enough to say the same forgot the time entirely.

1.2.2.0

No hope to recall only hope to fall through & at some time
all shall be well enough not that I believe any such thing only
the approximate curve of the geodesic equations subject to quantum
    corrections
I don't know any way to calculate being comforted by incompletion.

11:17 am. Partly cloudy. Partly cloudy for the hour.
A deficit. A neglect. An unidentified rage & a closed door, a locked door.
An imaginary door or the letters that spell a door like memory
an event or a neighbourhood or a trajectory sometimes inarticulate

annunciation of nothing by nothing still
"that we are sound, substantial, made of flesh & blood"
children's voices because they were children
& it was autumn & there was a kingfisher—

Because of its generality, this theorem does not tell us
whether the singularity will be in our past or in the future of our past.
The foreign necessary & no prayer & not much art or scope
left behind unordered reflections turning into the abstract double
    helix of migraine—

1.2.2.1

Displacement or caesura the streets all about
pavement, cobblestones & green trolley cars
no longer modern for example 2:36 pm overcast
paint on paint on paint becoming vertigo

& the small change in flavour, a sharper maybe, iron.
But who to tell unless you meet that revise
in the fog in a place you don't know.
They say there's nothing to remember after that.

Not ashes or briar or a definite edge
lost in detail which is a certain common grey exterior
oil paint meaning for example there aren't very many hardware stores.
3:09 pm. Overcast for the hour & snow until tomorrow morning.

Vicious slices & shards all edges
small sparks you keep finding for weeks
"in the dark time of the year. Between melting & freezing"
sight. Like that. Or even a waterglass.

1.2.2.2

Making any decisions & what we still call lamplight
has changed not vividly the all clear
to keep a record & this is not a record
wreckage piled to make a mountain.

The initial singularity
falling & disappears in the dry cold air sublimation.
This melody (listen!) slowly & then again
an action continuing in the present

no one following memory rewritten pools at the curb where there
    should be reflections—
emotion tangled up in cool not colour / scatters.
In the asthmatic present hard enough to anticipate the end of a line.
More difficult than coming through nothing.

Cold rain too the bare tree on Crawford Street
directions not a guide not definitive
the approximate curve of the geodesic equations subject to quantum
    corrections
introduce arbitrary coordinates on the 3-dimensional surface.

1.2.2.3

This has changed not vividly the all clear
moments close to touching hold without
grasping in devotion like the raven or kingfisher.
3:52 pm. Sunlight through leaves & shadows

apples again, sliced up now, angle of each cut
slightly different & a small change in flavour
sharper maybe, after you've pared away, or water
"to become renewed, transfigured, in another pattern"

after a fall, & in order: a landscape, a ghost, a reflection,
an epiphany. How to answer that? With leaving,
so loss creates & holds what is lost.
So & always information, decay.

An immersion is said to be an imbedding
if it is a homeomorphism onto its image
in the induced topology. A map, a proper map,
so the submanifold may not intersect itself.

1.2.3.0

If this is never spoken of if this didn't happen.
If matter curves space & space tells matter how to move.
If you move & there are ruins & ruins.
If I interrupt myself—

No site or formal counterpoint no machine of time
variation & associative logic beyond constraint
"at the moment which is not of action or inaction"
the same & not the same a path of scatters—

Impossible to see time.
11:05 am. Light snow for the hour.
Only trees threading light netted by the wind.
What wasn't found.

A field of poppies perhaps each seed point drawn out
a thread all the threads twisted a moving skein
knitted or knotted or woven with no pattern or vanishing—
Mark time along each one. Learn to draw like that.

1.2.3.1

The beginning is delight again.
Joy of it endless, embodiment
"of motives late revealed, & the awareness"
of joy is not joy but can perhaps

this close to the end come back to it
or leave pages blank nothing uncovered
neither noise nor silence uncertain bright
midday unopened books unfinished doubt

rewritten from memory beginning the apple tree the tree
on Crawford I see from my window writing is a maple of course
imagining apple tree branches bare the same way the same network not
the same shape but similar enough to say the same forgot.

For simplicity consider only the empty space
but similar arguments hold in the presence of matter
fields which obey well-behaved hyperbolic equations.
3:52 pm. Mostly cloudy for the hour.

1.2.3.2

New cathedral windows colour & colour
"of love beyond desire, & so liberation"
& apart of light. History scraped away.
Memory still rehearsed & mistaken.

Tone of voice but not words.
Action completed in the past or action
continuing in the present life.
Feather of breath on skin

unacknowledged experience unspoken for
resists narrative to leave breathing in & breathing out
3:50 pm sunset at 4:51 pm overcast for the next hour
& rain this evening full moon above the clouds

1:28 pm. Light snow for the hour & quiet
starlight falling into a well becoming violet with falling
snow fills the air this way then that way & the way
up is the way down always looks different.

1.2.3.3

There are no flowers & there
at them while they step back
not the same as coming to the end of it under Orion
a circle of folded slices of the night sky

where you can stand in the middle.
In the past as territories measure
a skinny dog sleeping by the millstone & the workshop's tumble.
They say there's nothing to remember after that.

If it is a homeomorphism onto its image
unreliable celebration a future almost reconciled
therefore enough to establish it in the preferred coordinate system.
The book will sag & melt, a dull pool & no stars.

More has been forgotten than a list, than a score.
A measure of the unpredictability of information content.
Small breakfasts, sometimes in the garden.
Present moment stretching if.

& if I interrupt myself
again or for the fifteenth time
written & whispered &
return & are nothing
near enough language
to say enough
you said more than once
ending in silence anyway
no response.
That can't be right.
What went—

& if I interrupt myself
again or for the sixteenth time
in the quiet of the rain
washing ash into gutters
grey stone quiet small
brittle thoughts returning to
the mother tongue remains
in all the outrage
still, another place, another time
lost. These things—

3

1.3.0.0

Same in the limit as it goes to infinity
the background changes (cat on the piano, empty coffee cup)
unremembered the detail edge past cutting.
Pour paint on all those pages. Go for a walk around the block

sans brilliant vision in sunlight morning.
What you want is explanation & at some time or point
infinite but another sense the wind takes them & the rain —
The long century broken into sentences or just broken.

A digression is in order.
Still down your tools compass square green mechanical
shadows may not be leaves
loss everyday snow melting in your palm.

A snowball thrown into the Grand Canyon by an 8-year-old
way down always looks different.
The topological fixed-point theorem.
Numbers. Arrival. A place. A real place. A site of thought.

1.3.0.1

The precarity of rubble without rhythm or self-similarity.
Places in the forest where bones surface 50 years after
the crime. Not here. Maybe a zipper pull. A rivet.
The gold nib of a fountain pen, ink-scaled.

Maybe an excess. Maybe better to say it
no more to say a matter of hearsay
scattered documents its own history
convenient forgetting & unasked for

briefly & just a page with its mechanisms & adornments
left over from coherent causal days patterned & directed.
"The detail of the pattern is movement"
not unlike breathing. That's past. Ink. 6:31 pm. Partly cloudy.

Time falls away or falls anyway geodesic
neither existent nor non-existent what is unknown
details leaving a general melancholia like sunlight
or prose. Redemption. War. Loss.

1.3.0.2

Not the same as coming to the end of it under Orion
throwing my keys off the bridge out onto the ice & walking away the
    damage
irreversible trajectory past & out falling further forward
sublime fragmented emptiness shards not even shards of the same thing

rewritten from memory beginning the apple tree the tree
on Crawford I see from my window writing is a maple of course
"the world becomes stranger, the pattern more complicated"
the same shape but similar enough to say the same forget the time entirely.

There's nothing special about these words.
Machine. Sparrow. Geodesic. Memory
of the precise colour of time deeper
rose blood rust heat eventually unreadable—

1:28 pm. Light snow for the hour & quiet
starlight falling into a well becoming violet with falling
snow fills the air this way then that way & the way
up is the way down always looks different.

1.3.0.3

As the falling clock slows we know incrementally
less & less let's say the frame shrinks around the clock
to an effective point lost information
that will survive the fall into infinitely compressed light—

unacknowledged experience unspoken for
resists narrative to leave breathing in & breathing out
3:50 pm sunset at 4:51 pm overcast for the next hour
& rain this evening full moon above the clouds

to consider loss when there was nothing
where grief should have been indeterminate geometry
sharp edges, diffuse shadows, breathing
thin memory if I interrupt myself

hollowing loss empty as feeling & always
"setting forth & not returning"
because there's no end to it & is that supposed to be a comfort?
There was a kingfisher. That's all.

1.3.1.0

"Or say that the end precedes the beginning"
home after a long day to feed the cat, like Philip Marlowe
neither a philosopher nor a war correspondent comfortable
in my sixth decade qualifying everything though.

Going further back this is what is given outside the windows a city writing
without clocks how small time is church bells & canonical hours
still down your tools compass square green mechanical
pencil burin Swiss micrometer no words but a tone of voice that fades—

Forgetting now & totally attentive
to it or say so is this
self-deception modernism
tangle complication delight entrance a glass staircase & granite cut
    incision

one voice or many, one then many
or many then one & singing, whispered, overheard
argument or conspiracy, perhaps endearments, seduction—
Lacework of quotation. Another notebook. 2:16 pm. Overcast.

1.3.1.1

In the absence of a metric
the Milky Way almost accustomed to it.
Questions themselves painful not thinking
one set. The haze that passes for clear sky.

When I was just winter streets
the memory of touch not touch still the memory of memory
is impossible even the memory of prayer.
Or buy old watches disassemble them & determine by practical
    observation

no tongues of flame. A small envelope containing
a deficit. A neglect. An unidentified rage & a closed door, a locked door.
It felt good to close the door
dividing the living from the dead, like snow.

Read again. Nothing beautiful. Gardens.
This is the centre of the century the pane of glass the rock
on the facing page sunlight edging through the blinds in bright triangles
2 rhythms & neither regular.

1.3.1.2

12:34 pm. Clear. Clear for the hour.
At this old pine table quiet street slight wind
from the north slight turning of the leaves knowing
at least I'll fill this page always one more thing.

Geometry & after pale light misinterpreted
a cloud of unknowing again
"at the recurrent end of the unending"
barren ground of memory language scraped away.

Time then unmetabolized imperfect betrayed by the fiction of precision
remembering clouds & no detail every clock
stopped the instant it comes into existence
only imagination & entirely present recall.

Maybe an excess. Maybe better to say it
no more to say a matter of hearsay
scattered documents its own history
convenient forgetting & unasked for.

1.3.1.3

Of history there alone & in company, in place
because you can't say what the place says
in anything like language the place shatters
refusing all motion & stillness at once all real places

"the only hope or else despair"
lost in detail which is a certain common grey exterior
oil paint meaning for example there aren't very many hardware stores.
3:09 pm. Overcast for the hour & snow until tomorrow morning.

Raining again there are 2 rhythms
steady rain rainwater running off the roof
2 rhythms & neither regular
that's what I want rain light rain —

The problem that words mean something
& this is a world of shards & stories
that can't be believed. Or finished. Even started
properly, picking up scraps & saying what or why —

1.3.2.0

Slow anniversaries mark the fixed frame
of life. Rewriting the same pages.
Not meaning but morning that fails
& fails again, no better for being / repeated.

No wristwatches stopped at random times
no brown paper & twine & wrapping paper
no photocopies of prints by Dürer vacation postcards or beach stones
no ticket stubs or pocket journal datebooks or cups full of coloured pencils
    & war poetry or volumes of the Stockholm edition of the works of
    Thomas Mann.

"When here & now cease to matter"
   apples again, sliced up now, angle of each cut
   slightly different & a small change in flavour
   sharper maybe, after you've pared away, or water

at the desk & making order of it
line by line or cell by cell knowing what you know.
Numbers. Arrival. A place. A real place. A site of thought.
Someone else has said this better.

1.3.2.1

A circle of folded slices of the night sky
in someone else's hand of questions
free of the past in the present repeatedly
6:01 pm. Partly cloudy. Partly cloudy for the hour.

Despite the constrained perspective & the lectern & the lion & the pen
the windowed room is empty the windows are empty
the scratching on the paper empty which is different than erased
which I have heard & still the lion growls or purrs in his radiant sleep

& this is the centre of the century the pane of glass the rock
"between three districts whence the smoke rose"
silence not ending it still & fire not ending it & ashes not ending it
every language burnt & written on air hot metal & dust

or the fox beside the lion there is a third picture that goes with these.
Not devotion or confession & without the force of ruins only numbers
for example the difficulty deducing the metric tensor from measurements
elegies multiply but how many ways to say broken glass—

1.3.2.2

All the old thoughts or just a thread.
Lacework of quotation. Another notebook. Time. Weather.
On Crawford I see from my window writing a maple of course
anchoring quiet it's possible to touch.

Light falls in this grain, these furrows.
Cold stars above empty fields. Thick stiff mud. Hoarfrost.
Exactly not remembered even if remembered
it scampers off just grey enough

words instead of feeling or real thought
this unopened text set aside & from memory
the compass & the book—
Then an airliner, & a car horn.

Dispossessed, abstract & unbodied the way mathematics is
generalizes itself to a tensor-valued one-form
fire without light or heat dark & pure burning
through uncertain windows even this comfort is no inside.

1.3.2.3

For example instead of a photograph
this melody (listen!) slowly & then again
or fast & then 1:35 pm. Snow. Snow for the hour.
Why is repetition necessary?

A prescription for attaching some kind of boundary
uniquely determined by measurements at non-singular points
to define at least a topology & possibly a differentiable structure & metric
an elegant formulation unfortunately very difficult to apply in practice

a field of poppies perhaps each seed point drawn out
a thread all the threads twisted a moving skein
knitted or knotted or woven with no pattern or vanishing—
Mark time along each one. Learn to draw like that.

If self falls apart in pebbles or bread crumbs
"quick now, here, now always"
an unravelling series a red thread beginning
the door on that maybe beginning—

1.3.3.0

Without edges & everything inside 12:56 pm light rain
there could be no memory poem obsession
no garden voices words not quite heard correctly
no returning or leaving either. Read carefully.

Something needs to interrupt me now.
A war. A shattered glass. Your eyes are still—
The fox turning back just look
"setting forth & not returning"

rewritten from memory beginning the apple tree the tree
on Crawford I see from my window writing is a maple of course
imagining apple tree branches bare the same way the same network not
the same shape but similar enough to say the same forget the time entirely.

Not there can't vanish it does
a snowball thrown into the Grand Canyon by an 8-year-old
falling & disappears in the dry cold air sublimation.
Incredible colour.

1.3.3.1

Revision stalls & interwoven tangles
like morning glories! that celestial blue! leaning
toward glorious luminary night & our early evening city
"the only hope or else despair—"

This happened then this happened.
The clock counting frame by frame
flattening event & memory, error
for the first time without time—

Remember. A small dog barking at the garbage collectors.
The cat sleeping on the piano again. Sun through the blinds.
12:41 pm. Partly cloudy. Partly cloudy for the hour.
All this, every object, field, connection to a past reaching out to futures all
    the sinews between them bunched here—obviously / stop.

Falling because falling is so complex it's simple [geodesic equation]
a fading tangle of loops & thread red thread & dried-up dark purple
again as if again memory is fallible who knew
a place we can walk through a house or a neighbourhood—

1.3.3.2

I don't know if silence is written by hand
a drawerful of stainless-steel cubes some with fine threaded holes
also small brass shims disordered & slippery with light machine oil
aphorism & scale independent error silences differ

figurative realist narrative description
anyway looking at them
"but heard, half-heard, in the stillness"
falling away. It never did.

The same again, don't remember
& you just can't get your hands on it.
A difference between a secret & an apple tree,
a love letter & bibliography, geometry, the fox at the roadside

when what are ashes or remembered
timepieces stopped broken willow shadows
washed by rain 10:57 pm & turbulence all
or some of the intermittencies of now revised—

1.3.3.3

Nevertheless despite these limitations one can still predict
filling time with pages instead
at this old pine table quiet street slight wind
a nest of propositions in the flames.

Free of the past in the present repeatedly
but similar arguments hold in the presence of matter,
thought, intent, grace, silence, mind, truth,
a fox at the roadside at sunset.

At the trestle table beside the high windows the fox & the lion —
But who to tell unless you meet that revise
in your own body maybe how you stand or walk your gait
tired of images only leaves you with

experimental tests of general relativity.
Language of forms.
Dynamics & some of their ramifications.
Today being today again, black, violet & —

& if I interrupt myself
again or for the seventeenth time—

& *if here, interruptions of absence,*
that is to say presence, present
sometimes looking over
your shoulder, the third person, that ghost
from another poem.
(Don't speak of it.)
A proofreader's mark.
A metaphysics. An immanence.
It's different now, after all
these years, how
could it not be & not
poems at all only these
correlated words entangled
words & time enough even
if these are words you'll
never —

& *if after this*
this & every ampersand continuing
another poem that can't
make up its mind & you
were there for all that
(farewell to all that)
(in parentheses)

(&c)
but none of them
only the fragments after
broken glass
a country road a tree
unnameable
others—

& *if I said it was like*
being in a room without windows, doors & then
there you are in the garden (almost winter garden) not
that you ever found the way out
but this is outside wind
& leaves. Not Jerome's room, Dürer's room,
table & books, *vanitas,*
memento mori &c
either, words refused
recognition & following, reminders & responsibilities.
Tear the pages out or add them
to the memory palace.
Your heart.

& *if I can't count them all, had not*
thought death had undone so many:
which poem is that? Not mine, none of yours.
Martyrs & new martyrs maybe
but this isn't martyrdom these words
faithless. The fox, again. We disagreed. In time
we disagreed further, or more.
We didn't understand a thing & everything
recurred, in the wrong place at the wrong time
but that's just how it is, isn't it?
Or how it was.

& *if now, here, a different city a city*
that was everything for you for
a while its avenues of monuments
to failure to sadness to being
unable to touch anything
or anyone &
that first glimpse
of ruins & fire
I wonder now
did you think
"my life will shut very beautifully, suddenly"
or did you think at all?
The myth of closure, repair, redemption, return.

& *if in the quiet of broken buildings*
in the quiet of the rain
washing ash into gutters
grey stone quiet small
brittle thoughts returning to
the mother tongue remains
in all the outrage
still, another place, another time
lost. These things together
define a distance, years. A net
of cities, rubble.

& *if I can walk away from this now*
the way you all must have walked halfway
across Europe in the dark
in the cold away along broken
roads almost
alone. Diaspora never regathered.
Worn-out decades you walked
toward, & yes
you are so many still & still
walking. Never
went back. Left
language there as well.
But the fox paused, bordering.

& *if here, surrounded by words*
written & whispered &
"you that shall cross from shore to shore years
hence are more to me, & more in my meditations
than you might suppose—"
return & are nothing
near enough language
to say enough.
"All language is meaningless"
you said more than once
ending in silence anyway
no response—
That can't be right.
What went wrong for which of us?

& *if you turn the pages, searching, find*
"Where now? Who now? When now?"
leaving us then at the right time perhaps
but who's to judge but you
"no matter how it happened."
To tangle all those or these times
we tried
maybe we tried & made
time for a while from the tangles

picking up pieces scraps & torn
postcards & library cards &
typewriter ribbon & only now
seeing myself all wrapped in
my self "by aporia pure & simple"
then & now how can I forget?
"Clear a space for it" you said.

&— *if then the now*
unneeded & unnecessary
paper set alight, simple quick foxfire &
ashes on the sand. I'm not sure
I've got the numbers right. "It seems
to me it was none of my doing."
Did I show you the photograph
of stones & metro tickets on the grave?
Repeating
there by accident, I. Don't remember.

& *if these things, these*
words & deaths & words, intertwine?
Scattered like sand, art. No, more.
Our times lacking ritual & the tragedy
we pretend otherwise. Out of these
splinters raise
a window, random pain
& shattered light shredded paper
as if the cathedral floor carpeted
in prayer but all we had were poems.
Some worse than others.

& *if the sky above open*
roof trees burnt-out forest
that could have been a city.
Lay in ruins writing. Read
silence. Don't speak
of it. Learn another
language instead or quote again "so
it is I who speak all alone
now."

& *if present or past, neither*
   portrait nor repetition,
   black nor white, some
   early flowers:
   one (no, all)
   of them — exquisite.
   Always the straightest line
   possible between perhaps
   there are gaps
   beginning delight always.

& *if time past every*
   uncertainty
   as in
   when did I know what
   & what
   do I know now this
   net of not
   knowing now
   unknowing
   as it frays, comes
   apart in my hands
   as if a fragile
   ornament

(a universe)
abandoned
garden you walked in
remembering, remembering
voices you knew
you'd heard somewhere else or
someone told you
of hearing them
or you or us or me or
no one.

& *if more words receding, shifting*
  "through reds she nears"
you said meaning
"redemption"

what

"relinquished speech"

then—

& *if time past & time future*
   retreat in requiem
   leaving us now
   suspended, unredeemable in
   these unreal years & lifetimes
   & how long
   till I forget your voice.
   Have I forgotten
   your voice?

& *if then*
you start at the beginning or start
at the end: you have to start
& you have to end. The motion
is its own music
& you can say dance to
the end. Swing time to
the end, & some times
the clock is fast & sometimes
the clock is slow & sometimes
standing still (in the quiet)
standing still (in the dark)
standing still (at the start)
is where it (or you) begin & end.
You have to start & you have to end.

& *if becoming less than loss*
is something you have
to hold on to, time
like the snow angled
from the north like
the rain angled from
the east, no memory
or need of memory

losing everything at once
beyond recollection, reconciliation, release:
small fragile folded bones
gasping for air just
beyond grasp, quiet as
the rain, the snow,
the wind's unthought words
naming the nothing left.

& *if to explain*
but these are not poems
you said a wind
of words from the past blowing
us into the now, new
angles all of us listening
who can hear dictionaries & encyclopedias:
all, complete, eternity—
be careful with this message.
There is no explanation.
There is no real explanation.
In some geometries you can
replace everything complicated
that happens everywhere
with something else, pure surface.
It's that simple but is it true?

&⸺ *if so I have to go back to this.*
Maybe it means nothing to you.

Or meant nothing.

(What is nothing?)

At this time I'm left with a lot of paper

& lists of words

still, often, realize, empty &c

& that's not quite the same

as unbounded or boundless the boundary

of a boundary is

the description

of a description

is awareness is

where does

the line

break—

the living & the dead &

after this silence then

who will stop who

will listen now

there is no one

here the empty room.

& *if the full stop matters*
more than the continuation or
is it easy to ignore time's
signature — is that it?
For the time being
let me sign this
circle an empty
circle or broken
circle approximation
& hesitation
incompletion
the sigh that becomes
wind falling over
cliff to the bay & the waves
below so easy
sometimes
I almost remember
the lines —

& *if a theory of loss or losing not*
just loss itself. How loss is written
on the edge of everything, a library
arranged in order after
the fact. Fitting the facts,
predictive & sensible, that

there was a reason for all this, that
we'd like to believe. The same
way clouds bloom sky flowers.
Bright dust & fog beyond
space & time.
Correlated.
You need a theory of loss or history.
You need a theory of order.
You need a theory of space & time, cause & effect.
You need a theory.

& *if now after*
all this time all
these frozen years & liquid
attempts to feel & think
it through despair
at everything undone
every letter unwritten meeting
missed all
our tools scattered
words scattered only
other people's books
I don't like to write in them
hoping to remember
all I've forgotten —

&   *if the numbers meant*
     there was use in them
     rows columns & diagonals
     summed to significance
     decrepit so-called science
     stranding us in Beauty.
     Plain to see.
     No predictive value
     outside the frame of chance.

&   *if the inside being the outside in*
     which I interrupt myself
     inevitably, pictorially
     asking if this
     descriptive or prescriptive purity presents
     "mercy & relaxation & even a strength"
     the skein followed
     back to an early evening,
     park bench, trees, towers
     of the city across the former
     ravine not quite filled in
     (a gap) but that belongs
     elsewhere, belongs
     to you even if you didn't
     take it with you, even

if I said please you
have to go, & you went.
There is a geometry
of regret also moving slowly
imperceptible shade of red
or should I say auburn,
dawn-coloured fire.
The fox in the half-light.

& *if without time no*
   memory, no recollection no
loss & no separation
boundary
&c
the words once written always
there
a wall tilting
after winter
after
time & memory—

Which book to write this in?
Serenity, equanimity, going easy—

& *if I interrupt myself*
    again, here, now
    the thought that this
    angel is also terrifying
    despite history & the theory of it even
    immanent experience all
    the monumental
    useless artwork
    lifework bodywork & none
    of it left now, these lines
    like any other useless
    writing or
    curve marked out by some compass or falling mass
    no matter how often
    repeated
    only the one loss.

& *if*
this broken elegy these broken
lines all broken
as if as if
I didn't care or it didn't
matter
all the dead broken emptiness
informed
by care did I care
& this broken performance
of it
fails, fails utterly
impossible as
love seems & it seems
broken as the ruins of
cities & words & minds & bodies
shattered at the roadside
silent, broken, even
if the fox turned, looked straight
at us (no, me)
& walked away.

& *if later not enough to begin & not*
enough to end there
say a bell with a rope
pull
tied off somewhere to the right out
of the frame
but now put your tools down again
without rage, impatience &c
deserving respect maybe
thinking, quiet thought
scattered
every time it almost
condenses.

& *if nothing to hold*
on to, absence
interrupted & broken but
hazy, voices in the fog
divorced from distance, short
lines like rain.
People with newspapers creased
over their heads in the downpour
on the bridge
in an old picture.
Cause & effect.

& *if, still, it's almost done*
for now
even if (say it!) it
will never be. Awkward
to admit you aren't getting it.
You? At this table again as
twilight thickens, more lines
scratched by hand, wrong again:
they flow: nothing like scratching
& remembering Blake's desire
for definite edges but
there's not much of him
here, it's all vague & even
if repeated still
unclear, not that
there are pieces missing (there are)
but the whole idea—

that you've got it wrong.
Saying there is no coherence but dreaming
of the ruins of
a vast beautiful broken
structure
redeemed by its ruination
when all the pieces never
came close to fitting together—

Even that's too much explanation.
Remembering the fox again,
realizing you haven't got a clue
& don't feel
anything oh & did you ever?
As if as if
affect was supposed to cohere (that word)
& how long
is a moment just a moment now
the memory of fire is not—
but burning—
to follow the rising sparks up
with the smoke & the shimmering
stars & trace
the transformation of red coals to grey ashes—
no one is that patient—

I've often given up.
Will again.
It doesn't matter how
I feel about it afterwards
I'll forget eventually everyone will.
What to do with all
this then?

Is that it that's not it.

&   *if almost done*
       obviously unfinished, provisional
       as it was always going to be
       a few fragments retrieved from
       what?
       No one to answer that.
       No one to ask.
       Telling myself once —
       but memory is doubtful
       unreliable &
       I don't trust what I want to believe.
       Order or chaos, order
       in chaos
       probability & determinism
       pulling at either end of our thread
       stretched over the abyss.
       Just breathe.
       Look across.
       Look down.
       If I could ask you
       any of you —

& *if of course it doesn't*
mean anything but that
doesn't mean it isn't
beautiful. Again:
is that all?

In another century all this
will be far away as
Troy
or the oak tree in the garden
the cypress in the courtyard
&c
equally unrepresentable, unthinkable
shatter of colours or mainly
green-grey (heaven-grey, heart-grey)
though I think
no one will ask.

    & if you wanted language
    to dance
      over cliché like fox-flame like

"a wreath, it is of"

      scattered parts
      interrupted
      uncompleted sentences

      of a book beginning & ending
      & a life soon after,
      then another.

    & if now these
    "20 years largely wasted"
      or has it been longer, much longer,
      & did that first war ever end or echo
      into all the others, forward & back, past
      & future haunted, "a different kind of failure"
      as you have it 2 lines later writing
      of a different matter, time, art, I only
      wish I could follow, here, in the middle way
      standing still, trying to stand still, trying
      to say I remember you, both

of you, all of you, although
that will crumble & scatter too
in the wars of the past & future &
the deaths of the past & future &
uncompromising silence left, held
in our empty hands—

& *if this city the bridge*
over rails & rails & new where
the lake was
a tree, a fox
wandering under old concrete
piers only a hint
of what was never built &
what was fortification &
how you followed through
the old ward / drawing
& monuments
never built
& railcars full of shattered men
& ghosts of women
you loved (I loved)
unset type or broken type
& the perfect
ampersand—

&   *if everything incomplete repeated*
    but how to build after or
    gather the shards simply put
    them in a drawer. No need
    to label it. No joy therein.
    Likewise no romance or terror
    of silence, language
    speaking us. Listen!
    No, it's nothing. The thrush
    is quiet, or gone. The city
    is quiet, the streets we knew
    together empty. So much
    left out, diachronic,
    synchronic, the wild fox.
    All there in every part.
    What if there really was
    a story behind these
    repeated nothings? What then?
    Just these glimpses —

&   *if not ignoring cause & effect*
      despite absence your effect.
      Dispersed, scattered, ashes, fog.
      Will we meet some hours
      before dawn
      in some shattered city silence
      it's not silence. The music
      you never heard. Every note
      filled with nothing, a melody
      a rhythm & how is that not
      a promise. We made no promises.
      An understanding to read perhaps.
      Some more words. Never finished &
      never to be finished.

&   *if "the truncation, the suggestion"*
      that sudden gust of wind
      scattering it all, or, insubstantial,
      the failed hard drive, the forgotten
      encryption key. Nothing to be done.
      So the strange durability of paper.
      Dog-ear this page. Remember me.
      I don't know how to wrap this up.
      Fold it over & see.

& *if the not knowing is central, the hints followed*
by guesses, allegations, the rest unheard songs uncaused
effects. Climb the hill & find the fox again.
I didn't follow, the first time or the last.
Left out all the names.
Some are more beautiful than others.

In ancient times lived & taught on this mountain
& there are no mountains here a lake &
now ravines filled in & streams buried
shore cliff, esker, glacial till—
A different teaching & the same.

& *if there now too many ideas*
objects withdraw prayer impossible
but sometimes a few.
The others also probability ghosts
into cloud grey preferring what tradition remains
when I was only capable of living in the past
I wish I could leave I didn't.
You can only wait so long. All at once.

& *if clocks fast / slow / in phase & slipping time*
because they can be erased or rearranged anyway
as if it could all burn away with how the words differ
when the rain doesn't have edges either.
A quotation could go here. Your choice. It's fading.
No presence because everything. Rules & exception.
This isn't progress but more comfortable
no longer modern for example
messianic & Miltonic this our city becomes
sleep or awakening.
Does art demand verisimilitude & who cares?
This is prose isn't it? Sometimes?
There was a kingfisher. That's all.
Or the fox also.

Where you lived & where I lived
time that time fall
into stories when there are no stories.
Well I'm thinking the time up
wanting static / wanting a frame
& not rain slipping how many times —

& *if what did I write?*
Not a question of faith or grace
& no agony getting there. Cold stars
another version of that story
their ghosts silent or at least —

Other people wrote down her name. His. Theirs.
O word! The contradiction (against the word)
of translation read
& is it singing, whispered, overheard,
falling only faintly —
There's no end.
Time. Secrets. Suspicion. Clamour.
Another country, where visitors were frequent
& the comfort of banality more tempting.

& *if impossible to finish here, perhaps*
start there now.
I thought I saw something in your eyes.
Abandon it. Or her, him, them.
Is that what I did that's
what I did. Admit lost time
revising light cast freely & unconstrained
without crossing out the rose garden either
again. Less. Still. Life. That.

A tangle of neurochemistry & intention
to say I don't feel much at all
in rough outline. If I think
it just goes on maybe I felt that way
never made things up chose not to say
there must be more to this, a story
that exists without you
& the numbers there's another one maybe
a cloud of unknowing again
after enough years
& fire above & around the flames
the fox at the roadside. Still. Dust. Letters.
Maybe it makes sense at the end there is no end.

& *if after negative theology is scraped clear*
the violence of enlightenment & heroic
being tilted in another direction (falling)
unsure of this like light the same & not the same
waking into unreasonable tears unmended
frame by repeated frame an essay or a best guess
perhaps if the form will carry through the garden
mountain laurel glossy, buried at least
after you've pared away, or snow then water
erase redraw write erase again quickly
conjectured not remembered & no reconciliation
but always another's words. Atonement.
What was that? Impossible covenant of. Repeated.

& *if there is no refusing time the remainder*
ending with time beginning
families we couldn't grow up in
families we couldn't grow up in
because 32 or 34 variations (a number) are not enough
so a list of losses at canonical hours left.
Drawing. Measuring. Writing now
a thread all the threads twisted radiant
starvation that left only pure grey
convenient forgetting & unasked for
names. To be reassured exist, consider grief

introjected & smoke thin rain cracking under empty
if this is a history then
not hierarchical dogma numbered parts & missing
because I don't have a story to tell beyond
I wanted to be
which is wrong. Ink dries quickly in the sun.

&   *if the hour on another timepiece or the sky*
remembers desire unvoiced hard to tell what's left.
Abandoned (almost winter). The living & the dead.
But the fox paused, bordering.
An error here to the end. No elegy or epitaph
only broken saying or doing nothing the noise
of accidents. Perhaps not even a poem.

& if I interrupt myself
again or for
are you counting
the eighteenth time—

14

2.0.0.0

Of history there alone & in company, in place
of regular solids, cone, polyhedron, calendar & timepiece
a positive constant of order unity given by
the *English Suites*? Calculations of the Riemann curvature tensor?

Action completed in the past or action —
That this is also love. That
we did that magnifying glass well mainly the corners
the sun's glare on this page until I adjust the blinds

retreat to reading echoes maybe another time.
It felt good to close the door.
Letters yet to be read or all burnt
but always another's words the beautiful

in the shape of grief not even prose.
Not even one cold full stop of feeling
salamander quick in the flames the coals ash jewelled eyes —
peacetime measured out into this revised future square of numbers.

2.0.0.1

Unending, unpunctuated by any equilibrium
but not chaotic / rules but not
one set. The haze that passes for clear sky.
Easy brokenness & rage without regret.

"To be conscious is not to be in time."
Desire or geometry is a conversation an orchestra
without recollection in the time it takes to read this.
The book should not have page numbers.

The fox beside the lion there is a third picture that goes with these.
Not devotion or confession & without the force of ruins only numbers
for example the difficulty deducing the metric tensor from measurements
elegies multiply but how many ways to say broken glass—

But oh! the slanting light & everything it connects anachronism.
More has been forgotten than a list, than a score.
Say what you see. That worked before. An hourglass.
Jerome at his translations, a drafty room in Nuremberg.

2.0.0.2

Like the river statistics like solutions to these equations
"the knowledge imposes a pattern, & falsifies"
unlike bones or metal insignia of rank
or even battalion records more than

the beginning is delight again.
Joy of it endless, embodiment
pure & outside time, & the memory
of joy is not joy but can perhaps—

A field of poppies perhaps each seed point drawn out
a thread all the threads twisted a moving skein
knitted or knotted or woven with no pattern or vanishing—
Mark time along each one. Learn to draw like that.

3:44 pm. Light rain starting later this afternoon.
Light rain off & on until Friday.
Always beginning out of time a chalkboard to make notes on wipe away
    clouds.
The line moves. The shadow moves. The time after.

2.0.0.3

Stars perhaps small holes burnt through paper as children
we did that magnifying glass well mainly the corners
watching white to cream umber ochre earth to black flame
no skill to put better words to those colours—

slow anniversaries mark the fixed frame
of life. Rewriting the same pages.
Not meaning but morning that fails
& fails again, no better for being / repeated

annunciation of nothing by nothing still
"the laughter in the garden, echoed ecstasy"
children's voices because they were children
& it was autumn & there was a kingfisher—

3:02 pm. Partly cloudy. Partly cloudy for the hour.
No constellations but the spiral turn of the hinged sky
is real or real enough cold of course the danger is
to fall into yourself & say nothing having felt nothing.

2.0.1.0

Hollowing loss empty as feeling & always
repeat myself & interrupt myself
because there's no end to it & is that supposed to be a comfort?
There was a kingfisher. That's all.

Although there is no pattern in the pattern
of the broken glass at the roadside
the detailed cross-hatching read as texture
not noise or a diamond cutting through

2:52 pm. Grey cold overcast & sunset at 4:44 pm.
Mechanical time. This then that. The stem
(like an apple) to set the time by reference
to another time or the sky / the escapement

a net of geodesics not causation self-similarity
"where past & future are gathered. Neither movement from nor towards,"
craters merging on the coast of ruins the rain pooling there
& the knives of window frames & the razors of stair treads & radiators &
    saucepans & coat hangers & each reflecting each—

2.0.1.1

Because there's no end to it & is that supposed to be a comfort?
For hours the world almost—
Sublime melancholy! Is that the remainder?
Lines crossed out.

Not there can't vanish it does
going further back this is what is given outside the windows a city writing,
sound of the river below unseeded. Not winter.
So the submanifold may not intersect itself.

Glimpse a fox in this civil twilight London say
without wires gears ailerons condensers just grey & some vibration
timepieces stopped broken willow shadows.
Dreaming a different garden, shady, an oak & an owl

when I was just winter streets.
Walk in the cold clear air & not
buy old watches disassemble them & determine by practical observation
no question of flame or purity, refined.

2.0.1.2

This happened then this happened.
The clock counting frame by frame
flattening event & memory, error
for the first time without time

a circle of folded slices of the night sky
in someone else's hand of questions
free of the past in the present repeatedly
6:01 pm. Partly cloudy. Partly cloudy for the hour.

Another's wordless ghost memory grieves
in your own body maybe how you stand or walk your gait
the memory of touch not touch still the memory of memory
is memory & you can forget something never remembered

broken sleet, uncertain & solitary & even that,
"that we are sound, substantial, made of flesh & blood,"
to be precise. Outlines can be enough
or haunting, nothing or everything / empty.

2.0.1.3

Is it enough or more than enough
to keep a record & this is not a record
small wind written by hand just disturbs
children watching airplanes dream.

"In the general mess of imprecision of feeling"
of the broken glass at the roadside
the detailed cross-hatching read as texture
not noise or a diamond cutting through

cold rain too the bare tree on Crawford Street
clearly visible fractal reach of its branches
as if the purpose of light in another city to
glimpse a fox in this civil twilight London say

where you can stand in the middle
11:55 am conjectured, unremembered, walk
or look down at the froth & flow, imagine
writing water & rocks, not even that in winter.

2.0.2.0

Cathedral window test pattern colour chosen by chance.
Inspiration. Shards of saints & stories blown apart—
in 1935, after the ruined country house in the company of—
at the trestle table beside the high windows the fox & the lion—

the compass & the book—
the materials enough in themselves
as the crack in the glass is part of it
as the shadow left or etched in the ruins, after poetry.

Light falls in these fields. Grain & furrows.
"Long hoped for calm, the autumnal serenity."
Stubble after harvest & highlight of first snow.
The sound of an airliner climbing over the wind.

Spatter, leopard, the starry sky or smallpox scar
& writing by hand living inside this
eating an apple 3:16 pm sunny
a roomful of light / a door—

2.0.2.1

Only now knowing insofar as it is possible
& perhaps in error & not empty not pure
sit & turn it over & over in your otherwise
empty hands never done with

a field of poppies perhaps each seed point drawn out
a thread all the threads twisted a moving skein
knitted or knotted or woven with no pattern or vanishing—
Mark time along each one. Learn to draw like that.

Maybe an excess. Maybe better to say
"we are sound, substantial, made of flesh & blood"
scattered documents its own history
convenient forgetting & unasked for.

1:59 pm. Mostly cloudy for the hour. Every equation an approximation
that undoes itself falling like space or each repetition is not noise
beginning again or not if there is no end the beginning
that voice these voices & how that implicates not enough / to continue—

2.0.2.2

Seed pods blown, dried after one winter,
argument or conspiracy, perhaps endearments, seduction—
Breathless & hopeful unbroken distance. Forgetting & retelling.
On Crawford I see from my window writing is

all shall be well enough not that I believe any such thing only
inarticulate now
in this place in this time maybe only
a yellow green ladder trade name Featherlite

or does desire stream through & cannot be recalled.
Starting to the rain slowing back to polyrhythms.
There are still a few pages left.
Children writing on a slate the book closed resting outside

oil paint meaning for example there aren't very many hardware stores
or listening the unthought knowing a tangle
of local Lorenz geometry & local Euclidean geometry
an event or a neighbourhood or a trajectory sometimes inarticulate.

2.0.2.3

10:25 am. Overcast. A key turning. Plain text. A door.
It's difficult to touch this exactly being erased
retreat to reading echoes maybe another time
I thought I saw something in your eyes.

It wasn't much. A bird speaking. A thrush
kingfisher or killdeer in the distance.
I wrote letters that were answered.
We spoke for hours. We still see each other sometimes.

"When time stops & time is never ending"
time slips & to measure it each alone
the child neglected in overwhelming
or waking in an empty house valuing solitude

the background changes (cat on the piano, empty coffee cup)
half full of wanting to or having wanted now learning maybe
here alone those moments it curls up tight coherent causal
I think Tom just perhaps but that passes.

2.0.3.0

Some darker clouds, light rain today through Wednesday.
2:24 pm. Without philosophy, occupation, charge, beyond
temporal order & forgetting or disorder & error
"& cold the sense & lost the motive of action"

in a fractal mesh of maybe & conditional present
tense experienced not reasoned intuition that
the wave function collapses again & again in melancholy geometry's
many repetitions / highest apple / tree or fox—

Probabilities don't compel, are only useful when action is repeated.
Not determined even if determinism can be predictable complex
in its strange attractions. Some deeper brighter transience.
Nothing up my sleeve except now a lion. (That trick never works.)

How the words differ when interrupted is memory / is time
& splendour! it did NOT cohere the better for it a lifetime spent
trying to say what's missing / mountains / high clear sky / curtained dusk
all of it returning desolation, angelic order or stage direction / A country
    road. A tree. / Evening.

2.0.3.1

"So here I am, in the middle way, having had 20 years"
  uniquely determined by measurements at non-singular points
  to define at least a topology & possibly a differentiable structure & metric
  an elegant formulation unfortunately very difficult to apply in practice

  & this is the centre of the century the pane of glass the rock
  hurled at the lightening cracks radiating before the slivers crash
  silence not ending it still & fire not ending it & ashes not ending it
  every language burnt & written on air hot metal & dust—

  as if it could all burn away with no question of pure ashes
  a field or a handful & in time falling far enough
  the trajectory & distribution having no unique source tree
  without roots or rooted in a cloud of unknowing only now

  your voice heard again in archived voice mail
  can't call you back breathless & hopeful unbroken
  at that beginning even if the fox knows gnawing on silences
  (3:10 pm. Overcast.) learning not to ask or indirectly.

2.0.3.2

"Lying awake, calculating the future"
in a rush for it to be over & then, now
will have a shape. Polyhedron.
A book beginning this & ending time, or burnt & one.

Cold stars above empty fields. Thick stiff mud. Hoarfrost.
The future & the past all empty. Dry stalks of Queen Anne's lace.
It would have been a meadow after,
before the cold, the presocratic fragments

the passage work & so much left
undone unlived self shattering into myriad
bright prism points all across the floor
at your feet papers in the wind imagine one copy—

The problem that words mean something
& this is a world of shards & stories
that can't be believed. Or finished. Even started
properly, picking up scraps & saying what or why—

2.0.3.3

So nothing begins because the breath
& so shrines are built outside cause & effect
a net of geodesics not causation self-similarity
one voice or many, one then many.

Not even one cold full stop of feeling
forgetting now & totally attentive
no returning or leaving either. Read carefully
loss everyday snow melting in your palm.

In bent space counting time on incomparable watches
read again. Nothing beautiful. Gardens
of branching light & dark displaced covariant derivatives.
Watch each thought's trajectory through time as memory ravels round
   itself

the selves lived, stains on a shirt you thought was clean
& you just can't get your hands on it.
Wind bending the trees in the east burning information.
Quickly. Tell repeatedly nothing at all nothing.

& if I interrupt myself
again or for the nineteenth time
this & every ampersand continuing
another poem that can't
make up its mind & you
were there for all that
(farewell to all that)
(in parentheses)
(&c)
but none of them
only the fragments after
broken—

& if I interrupt myself
again or for the twentieth time
that is to say presence, present
sometimes looking over
your shoulder, the third person, that ghost
from another poem.
(Don't speak of it.)
A proofreader's mark.
A metaphysics. An immanence.
It's different now, after—

2.1.0.0

Sky falling along every geodesic
no brown paper & twine & wrapping paper.
There is anger. There is a war. A tearing. A dislocation.
Outside accurately scattered the same way—

I feel alone & too much I
in a rush for it to be over & then, now
joy of it endless, embodiment
deep sapphire in a book.

In the induced topology a map, a proper map,
reminding myself that I can delete this rewrite substantially—
red thread / orange / terrible blue white now without now & no memory
    of it—
no longer modern for example time & weather.

A workshop, but nothing is built there.
There was a kingfisher. That's all.
Apples dried up into sketches.
Time then unmetabolized imperfect betrayed by the fiction of precision.

2.1.0.1

Beginning with a place or with the end not beginning
"setting forth & not returning"
not order or intermittent emptiness beginning
outside accurately scattered the same way—

Perhaps there are gaps.
To preserve, to elevate, to cancel.
No time to find out stopping
means more than already 8:06 pm

not to dwell on this regret or move on
to polygons & scattered tools / compass & closed book
different from the moment you're certain you're out of the woods across
 the frontier all clear
then we came forth to see again the stars.

Do I refuse recollection or is there nothing to remember?
A thrush was singing but it's quiet now.
Far-off construction. A power saw.
Then an airliner, & a car horn.

2.1.0.2

Nevertheless despite these limitations one can still predict
today being today again, black, violet &
the occurrence of singularities under certain conditions.
What was the weather like, the crossing?

1:28 pm. Light snow for the hour & quiet
starlight falling into a well becoming violet with falling
snow fills the air this way then that way & the way
up is the way down always looks different.

OK, self shatters & the shards are dangerous still
"we are sound, substantial, made of flesh & blood"
interrupted by hawk migration in cloudless sky the self presented here &
the selves lived, stains on a shirt you thought was clean

accumulation over years & unsymmetric silence
which means what? Zero or broken glass coming after
more difficult than coming through nothing
to push against cold dust questions unasked unformed vague unease—

2.1.0.3

Red thread ties the hours not
a fabric or a net not that
regular looking back to see
causes or the singularity of forgetting.

No wristwatches stopped at random times
no brown paper & twine & wrapping paper
no photocopies of prints by Dürer vacation postcards or beach stones
no ticket stubs or pocket journal datebooks or cups full of coloured pencils
   & war poetry or volumes of the Stockholm edition of the works of
   Thomas Mann.

Water over rocks & what's left of the mill a constant distribution
of frequencies of froth & foam the result of runoff from farm fields
"into different lives, or into any future"
a catenary arc is not a parabola it's weighted down

ending with time beginning
with sunrise moonrise 5:40 am 5:49 pm clear
aircraft overhead / traffic / air conditioners / rhythm
of electrical demand / power factors / naive presence —

2.1.1.0

Voices from the street not my language. The thrush again. Sparrows.
The quiet is important why is the quiet important.
Answering. Not a sound. Listen higher everywhere
tinnitus of the quantum vacuum massed choir—

your voice heard again in archived voice mail
can't call you back breathless & hopeful unbroken
at that beginning even if the fox knows gnawing on silences
learning not to ask or indirectly.

11:17 am. Partly cloudy. Partly cloudy for the hour.
A deficit. A neglect. An unidentified rage & a closed door, a locked door.
An imaginary door or the letters that spell a door like memory
an event or a neighbourhood or a trajectory sometimes inarticulate

"has answered light to light & is silent, the light is still."
Home after a long day to feed the cat, like Philip Marlowe
neither a philosopher nor a war correspondent comfortable
in my sixth decade qualifying everything though.

2.1.1.1

An immersion is said to be an imbedding,
how thought comes into mind or memory & arcs out
the trajectory & distribution having no unique source tree
walking in winter under Orion to buy books

again & again every diamond cut into.
The time doesn't matter as much now. Urgency has drained away.
This has changed not vividly the all clear
from the north slight turning of the leaves knowing

incredible colour.
As the falling clock slows we know incrementally.
Time. Weather. A key turning. Plain text. A door.
I see I forgot the apple also

how much hope doesn't matter. A crystal palace collapsing—
Not determined even if determinism can be predictable, complex.
They say there's nothing to remember after that.
There's nothing special about these words.

2.1.1.2

A prescription for attaching some kind of boundary
uniquely determined by measurements at non-singular points
to define at least a topology & possibly a differentiable structure & metric
an elegant formulation unfortunately very difficult to apply in practice

"in windless cold that is the heart's heat"
if self falls apart in pebbles or bread crumbs
an unravelling series a red thread beginning
the door on that maybe beginning—

Without a picture new names slipping
only tall & east & raven & field grey uncertain fog
unknowing as children as displaced
children home is where

an action continuing in the present
that continuity the assumption taking up past
& future memory rewritten but not all
the rewriting replacing hours & hands, some empty—

2.1.1.3

All is not lost. To wonder what grace this leaves us with
what tradition remains to be unfolded & reread
what value & answering the sleepers in the underground
blacked-out windows & the few walking dark streets

12:39 pm. Mostly cloudy. Mostly cloudy for the hour.
Devote yourself to calculation, enumeration
not the same as memory or a book or a wristwatch.
There are still a few pages left.

"In the uncertain hour before morning"
old loves & current to address, letters, on paper
real & all of it properly radiant life / beautiful desire / gift
of everything I do not have & cannot—

If you shatter into 1,000 (& one) stories
children playing in the street this afternoon
& singing (that's rare) in discordant concord
interrupted by reply & post arriving.

2.1.2.0

Turn the page. Memory is fire in its cabinet
fire without light or heat dark & pure burning.
The book will sag & melt, a dull pool & no stars.
Unrecalled therefore unrepeated. Unnumbered. One one one.

Remember. A small dog barking at the garbage collectors.
The cat sleeping on the piano again. Sun through the blinds.
12:41 pm. Partly cloudy. Partly cloudy for the hour.
All this, every object, field, connection to a past reaching out to futures all
    the sinews between them bunched here—obviously / stop.

Repetition is interruption sometimes avalanche
the smell of death unforgettable revolting sweetness
but time has no scent no trace is framed by memory
"sound, substantial, made of flesh & blood"

irregular, small enough to hold & polished
so you can see yourself in its pitted facets.
4:16 pm. Mostly cloudy. For the hour.
In the shape of grief not even prose.

2.1.2.1

How the words differ when interrupted is memory / is time
& splendour! it did NOT cohere the better for it a lifetime spent
trying to say what's missing / mountains / high clear sky / curtained dusk
all of it returning desolation, angelic order or stage direction / A country
    road. A tree. / Evening.

"In the dark time of the year. Between melting and freezing"
revision stalls & interwoven tangles
like morning glories! that celestial blue! leaning
toward glorious luminary night & our early evening city

broken sleet, uncertain & solitary & even that
is wrong, the word wanted is *relinquish*
to be precise. Outlines can be enough
or haunting, nothing or everything / empty.

5:34 pm. Light rain for the hour.
Time slips & to measure it each alone
the child neglected in overwhelming
or waking in an empty house valuing solitude.

2.1.2.2

Time. Without philosophy, occupation, charge, beyond
& before the cold, the presocratic fragments
the question of burial remains & if elegy
shadows may not be leaves

paint on it what self-portrait tree skeleton grid—
a field or a handful & in time falling far enough.
Unreliable time in a froth of emptiness.
Now leaves dry & about to having

imagined light tracking abstract across white walls
a skinny dog sleeping by the millstone & the workshop's tumble
no one following memory rewritten pools at the curb where there should
    be reflections—
empty hands never done with.

A deficit. A neglect. An unidentified rage & a closed door, a locked door
exactly not remembered even if remembered.
How often again looking at them & looking.
The cat sleeping on the piano again. Sun through the blinds.

2.1.2.3

At a certain point in time the cost of memory
exceeds the cost of never knowing & everything—dishes, scissors,
    perfume bottles, shoe racks, magazines, Chinese rugs, salt, luggage,
    silhouettes, leaf rake,
the I don't know & that's the point—
"to become renewed, transfigured in another pattern—"

Light falls in these fields. Grain & furrows.
No abandoned country churches, worn-away gravestones, overgrown
    rosebushes.
Stubble after harvest & highlight of first snow.
The sound of an airliner climbing over the wind.

Light shifts. Light slants, conciliate or another word
for what light could say falling
light as fast as possible the ruin of time
no matter how beautiful go looking for shadows

of branching light & dark displaced covariant derivatives
life burnt away radiant life & no ash of words
on broken glass gravestones, thorn bushes growing.
2:38 pm. Partly cloudy for the hour.

2.1.3.0

Cloud of unknowing brief & always cloud
of forgetting that cloud shaped like
a continent a coastline foam left
by waves breaking before the next wave knowing

all they'll say decades later beginning partway down
a lifetime & still walking time & weather
unrecalled green leaves maybe no coat yet
I see I forgot the apple also.

"You cannot face it steadily, but this thing is sure,"
this melody (listen!) slowly & then again
or fast & then 1:35 pm. Snow. Snow for the hour.
Why is repetition necessary?

As if action were enough. What do you do after that, & after after?
Live alone with your line breaks? Paperweights? Apples? That fox?
The *English Suites*? Calculations of the Riemann curvature tensor?
Pour paint on all those pages. Go for a walk around the block.

2.1.3.1

Not the same as coming to the end of it under Orion
throwing my keys off the bridge out onto the ice & walking away the
   damage
irreversible trajectory past & out falling further forward
sublime fragmented emptiness shards not even shards of the same thing

the set of all points which can be reached
along integral curves from a given point
by the transformations generated by commuting vector fields
form an immersed 2-dimensional submanifold

alone. Without remembering or acting on memory.
Returning without memory this last time again.
At liberty. Before decision. In contemplation.
A pebble gathering speed only now again. 12:56 pm. Overcast.

Deity expands through us a wavefront of bliss radiant starvation
only pure grey bones left unburied ash of stars just stars & all the dark
   between
"ash on an old man's sleeve"
tired of paper tangled minds & scraps I believed that once—

2.1.3.2

The passage work & so much left
undone unlived self shattering into myriad
bright prism points all across the floor
at your feet papers in the wind imagine one copy

& rain 8:06 pm if remembering stained radio noise
coastline doubling back to television snow Orion
the first time to structure repetition no one taught me that raised
by a library of wolves fresh cave fox shadows —

There's nothing special about these words.
Machine. Sparrow. Geodesic. Memory
of the precise colour of time deeper
rose blood rust heat eventually unreadable —

Between deaths & gestures objects as raw as prayer
"accept the constitution of silence"
a skinny dog sleeping by the millstone & the workshop's tumble
measurement & perspective exception & rule I can't speak to.

2.1.3.3

Sit here with a book. The wind breathes.
There is no plan, just repetition. Another page.
Sharp edges, diffuse shadows, breathing.
Cities of rooftops & streets bare trees against the lovely blueness of
  twilight.

There are no flowers & there,
a difference between a secret & an apple tree,
the ashes of stories memories of fire & the sound of fire
small packages & precious improvisations

peacetime measured out into this revised future square of numbers
only see it & only at times / darkly.
Far-off construction. A power saw.
Redshift continued

& writing by hand living inside this.
Watch each thought's trajectory through time as memory ravels round
  itself.
No hope to recall only hope to fall through & at some time
sans brilliant vision in sunlight morning—

& if I interrupt myself
again or for the twenty-first time
unneeded & unnecessary
paper set alight, simple quick foxfire &
ashes on the sand. I'm not sure
I've got the numbers right.
Did I show you the photograph—

      & if I interrupt myself
again or for the twenty-second time
         silent, broken, even
if the fox turned, looked straight
             at us no
there are 22 words missing—

11

2.2.0.0

Scraping over it covering this time another stopped watch—
No beginning is the highest truth I've heard.
The background changes (cat on the piano, empty coffee cup):
the precarity of rubble without rhythm or self-similarity

different from the moment you're certain you're out of the woods across
    the frontier all clear
without memory rust or other words.
No abandoned country churches, worn-away gravestones, overgrown
    rosebushes.
Read this now. That word. Zero. What do you think?

Weak gravitational fields
continuing in the present life
should be or is it will have been
into the net of sky / not infinite / receding

words instead of feeling or real thought
making any decisions & what we still call lamplight
that will survive the fall into infinitely compressed light—
or many then one & singing, whispered, overheard.

2.2.0.1

Complex hierarchies fall away jewel by jewel
not a new idea ongoing like rain
with an undertone of ecstatic grammar
of the broken glass at the roadside.

Books reread returned to for comfort or provocation make a London in
　　the mind
left over after the fall & light in the windows
the approximate curve of the geodesic equations subject to quantum
　　corrections
vicious slices & shards all edges.

Time. Weather. A key turning. Plain text. A door
disappears in the dry cold air sublimation.
The delusion of black & white
evolves even with many documents destroyed paper

refusing all motion & stillness at once all real places
unreliable celebration a future almost reconciled
looking closely at the curl of small dimensions
into radiant pixels worthless like life also unfinished.

2.2.0.2

Over years & so the rose garden & everybody knows the ruined chapels
    country houses broken cities
the ashes of stories memories of fire & the sound of fire.
The *English Suites*? Calculations of the Riemann curvature tensor?
Properly, picking up scraps & saying what or why—

Time. By heart or memory not belief
is prose isn't it? Sometimes
that time is not temporal
& it was autumn & there was a kingfisher—

this unopened book set aside & from memory
leaf green plates on the table left outside.
Probabilities don't compel, are only useful when action is repeated.
Read: astronomy answers questions with evasion,

a snowball thrown into the Grand Canyon by an 8-year-old.
Do I refuse recollection or is there nothing to remember?
Not meaning but morning that fails
for answers if noise is indistinguishable—

2.2.0.3

Children's voices because they were children.
It wasn't like that. Ever. Steel & copper
& the possibility that even if one did it would still be insufficient.
Cold stars above empty fields. Thick stiff mud. Hoarfrost.

No more bright punctuation or shiny word-coins.
Always falling wind before the firestorms adding up histories
the compass & the book—
of familiar lines recalled & copying them out.

Forgetting now & totally attentive,
impossible to see time
tinnitus of the quantum vacuum massed choir—
like morning glories! that celestial blue!

Books reread returned to for comfort or provocation make
a one-parameter family of geodesics.
Then it curves & falls back to absence.
Broken concrete. Warm wood.

2.2.1.0

Interrupted by never getting past half empty now
deity expands through us a wavefront of bliss radiant starvation.
Pour paint on all those pages. Go for a walk around the block.
We spoke for hours. We still see each other sometimes.

But who to tell unless you meet that revise
throwing my keys off the bridge out onto the ice & walking away the
    damage
quick motion all corners in this cottage or gentrified row house
tearing deeply away. Real embodied equivalence.

Hard to mark beginning exactly interrupting myself with again,
without a theory of history, ruins, indifference —
to come or being lived through
watching white to cream umber ochre earth to black flame

if I rewrote from memory & forgetting
seed pods blown, dried after one winter,
memory encrypts itself & the key is lost I never —
The explanatory entropy on the wall.

2.2.1.1

In the induced topology, a map, a proper map,
for what light could say falling
only pure grey bones left unburied ash of stars just stars & all the dark
    between
that's what I want rain light rain—

writing water & rocks, not even that in winter.
I think Tom just perhaps but that passes.
Of conversion belief modernism even if it was a literature
here alone those moments it curls up tight coherent causal

speech an imposter unmarked by signs.
The neighbour's porch light on across the street.
Wet iron water seeping below roots hiding
& this is the centre of the century the pane of glass the rock—

The lane warm lit windows in the twilight woods torn clouds thin moon.
Books reread returned to for comfort or provocation make a London in
    the mind.
Annunciation of nothing by nothing still
that man & his books, or that child & the games—

2.2.1.2

Tangle complication delight entrance a glass staircase & granite
not noise or a diamond cutting through
matter implied by its effect on observables
left over from coherent causal days patterned & directed.

Maybe an excess. Maybe better to say
& no different disperse now & eventually
measures something. Time. Weather.
No whole these are parts of.

Desire or geometry is a conversation an orchestra
no returning or leaving either. Read carefully.
The image of the past decaying into noise time being
fire without light or heat dark & pure burning.

I feel alone & too much I
(like an apple) to set the time by reference
or the occurrence of singularities under certain conditions.
There is anger. There is a war. A tearing. A dislocation.

2.2.1.3

Not concerned not looking at old photographs or letters or emails,
the gold nib of a fountain pen, ink-scaled,
cathedral window test pattern colour chosen by chance.
A small plane passes over. Perhaps the thrush again but that's not so.

Mechanical time. This then that. The stem
rose blood rust heat eventually unreadable —
How the words differ when interrupted is memory / is time
the story is not the life / remembered.

Remember. A small dog barking at the garbage collectors.
If I interrupt myself —
filling time with pages instead
(like an apple) to set the time by reference

interrupted by hawk migration in cloudless sky the self presented here &
not determined even if determinism can be predictable, complex.
Feather of breath on skin
the child neglected in overwhelming —

2.2.2.0

Causes or the singularity of forgetting
pools of rain & mossy stones, colder, wetter days getting shorter
how it becomes cliché or stuck not dissolving,
always beginning out of time a chalkboard to make notes on wipe away
    clouds.

Only trees threading light netted by the wind
breathing porcelain & asbestos
at them while they step back
the trajectory & distribution having no unique source.

Wet streets after rain meeting no one,
what tradition remains to be unfolded & reread
all that's left of homecoming now.
No skill to put better words to those colours

self-deception modernism
means more than already time
from geometry & falling or falling. Drawing.
Unrecognized names wasted teleology or a diary.

2.2.2.1

The explanatory entropy on the wall
that time clear-eyed & immaculate
a circle of folded slices of the night sky
imposed by the desire for order another network.

Wet iron water seeping below roots hiding
if you are real or the children's voices.
Unlike grief this repetition the decision to copy
stopped the instant it comes into existence.

No question of flame or purity, refined
but there's no anger because anger is death that's right
lines crossed out
at least I'll fill this page always one more thing

& no different disperse now & eventually
not the same as coming to the end of it under Orion
having to live with these memories.
Maybe an excess. Maybe better to say.

                                    & if I interrupt myself
                       again or for the twenty-third time
                          that was everything for you for
                        a while its avenues of monuments
                            to failure to sadness to being
                                unable to touch anything
                                              or anyone &
                                         that first glimpse
                                             of ruins & fire
                                                I wonder now
                                                       did—

2.2.2.2

Stocked brown trout leaping parabolic geodesics remember.

Who lives there now? A character from an old book.

Peacetime measured out into this revised future square of numbers.

No ticket stubs or pocket journal datebooks or cups full of coloured pencils
   & war poetry or volumes of the Stockholm edition of the works of
   Thomas Mann—

all must pass through optical depth.

Incredible colour.

Time & weather.

Broken afterwards shell pits filled with rain or groundwater

& the small change in flavour, a sharper maybe, iron,

or even battalion records more than

a distant siren fire trash collection

your voice heard again in archived voice mail

causes or the singularity of forgetting

a fox at the roadside at sunset

called a fibre bundle which is locally

the materials enough in themselves—

2.2.2.3

A thread all the threads twisted a moving skein
not being able to say what is forgotten or not remembered not
in bent space counting time on incomparable watches
memory encrypts itself & the key is lost I never —

midday unopened books unfinished doubt
unlike bones or metal insignia of rank
inarticulate now
she played, chalk on sidewalk, Himmel oder Hölle, Angry Birds —

Incredible colour,
the scratching on the paper empty which is different than erased
is prose isn't it? Sometimes
light as fast as possible the ruin of time

leaf green plates on the table left outside
starting to the rain slowing back to polyrhythms
today being today again, black, violet &
bright prism points all across the floor.

2.2.3.0

A thread all the threads twisted a moving skein
a chain of alternatives unchosen / losses.
Red thread ties the hours not
balconies wooden stairs in the snow in another city still

but always another's words the beautiful
as yet the question how much is lost.
This undertaking requires a knowledge of
the occurrence of singularities under certain conditions,

growing up among foreigners our native
not the act itself or alone.
At this table scraps of the 20th century measured out.
Light falls in these fields. Grain & furrows,

children's voices because they were children
in more than one book not to be reconciled the book closed
as if you could choose to remember or forget
or wheels a sort of useless machine counting cannot be a poem.

2.2.3.1

The smell of death unforgettable revolting sweetness
to keep a record & this is not a record.
No time to find out stopping
& the small change in flavour, a sharper maybe, iron.

All is not lost. To wonder what grace this leaves us with
dividing the living from the dead, like snow.
OK, self shatters & the shards are dangerous.
A faded star, part of a reactionary

there are no flowers & there —
Scraps. Incompletions. Endings without beginnings.
No ticket stubs or pocket journal datebooks or cups full of coloured pencils
    & war poetry or volumes of the Stockholm edition of the works of
    Thomas Mann —
& the comfort of banality more tempting not fire.

Shadows may not be leaves
can be most easily examined by constructing a manifold.
Reading it all again requires return
from memory not life / by heart.

2.2.3.2

Some of the geometrical properties of a manifold—
what you want is explanation & at some time or point
no whole these are parts of.
Tinnitus of the quantum vacuum massed choir—

Not there can't vanish it does
all the old thoughts or just a thread
writing water & rocks, not even that in winter.
No path retraced eyes closed wanting not

what to do later today or tomorrow
unremembered the detail edge past cutting
time conjectured, unremembered, unremembered
matter implied by its effect on observables.

Lacework of quotation. Another notebook.
Seed pods blown, dried after one winter.
I wrote letters that were answered.
A yellow green ladder trade name Featherlite.

2.2.3.3

Its order only imposed by the desire for order,
fire without light or heat dark & pure burning.
It wasn't much. A bird speaking. A thrush.
Of history there alone & in company, in place.

Use these metric components & the components of
old loves & current to address, letters, on paper
in strange duty closing the door on ruins.
Another city in which strangers throng & buy

the delusion of black & white.
Light as fast as possible the ruin of time
at hand it scampers off just grey enough.
Not being able to say what is forgotten or not remembered not

the explanatory entropy on the wall
the same & not the same a path of scatters—
the trajectory & distribution having no unique source tree
& in the process disconnects its outer regions.

& if I interrupt myself
again or for the twenty-fourth time
but how to build after or
gather the shards simply put
them in a drawer. No need
to label it. No joy therein.
Likewise no romance or terror
of silence, language
speaking us. Listen—

& if I interrupt myself
again or for the twenty-fifth time
roof trees burnt-out forest
that could have been a city.
Lay in ruins writing. Read
silence. Don't speak
of it. Learn another
language instead or quote again
there are 5 words missing—

2

2.3.0.0

Chance falling together
hard to mark beginning exactly interrupting myself with again
as if it could all burn away with no question of pure ashes
tired of paper tangled minds & scraps I believed that once —

No site or formal counterpoint no machine of time.
Understanding something of it as it comes apart
half full of wanting to or having wanted now learning maybe
where grief should have been indeterminate geometry

& after that what does zero mean.
Geodesic grain & ashes of words mainly numbers
some left out after all those missing
this unopened book set aside & from memory:

Time. Weather.
Then its translation reads
no skill to put better words to those colours —
peacetime measured out into this revised future square of numbers.

2.3.0.1

Small tonal transitions of the black & white past
in another city of grey stones somewhat abstract
sometimes melancholy lacking mirrors
without a theory of history, ruins, indifference—

5:34 pm. Light rain for the hour.
Time slips & to measure it each alone
the child neglected in overwhelming
or waking in an empty house valuing solitude

action conditioned & dependent still life
without need recurs & varies unconcerned
unreliable celebration a future almost reconciled.
"The time of the seasons & the constellations"

emptiness itself & wind & forgetting possibly
a distant siren fire trash collection
remembering ash cans made of metal
grey galvanized past ringing details—

2.3.0.2

Living starlight paper geometry & secrets
tearing deeply away. Real embodied equivalence.
A nest of propositions in the flames.
Hold fast. 2:20 pm. Light snow.

Repetition is interruption sometimes avalanche
the smell of death unforgettable revolting sweetness
but time has no scent no trace is framed by memory
to say nothing, feel nothing, remember nothing, think

all they'll say decades later beginning partway down
a lifetime & still walking time & weather
unrecalled green leaves maybe no coat yet
I see I forgot the apple also

at the desk & making order of it
"its hints of earlier & other creation."
Numbers. Arrival. A place. A real place. A site of thought.
Someone else has said this better.

2.3.0.3

Embodied time runs strangely, irreducibly aporetic
(note, philosophers!) interrupted by kids on skateboards the street
is slightly downhill sound a trowel spreading cement
scraping over it covering this time another stopped watch—

Over years & so the rose garden & everybody knows the ruined chapels
    country houses broken cities
the feel & smell of an old book not death held open in 2 hands & for
    example on page 213
"hints followed by guesses, & the rest"
under fading dust wrappers sky blue cloth fine with no markings or
    annotations to return to.

Not a new idea ongoing like rain 5:28 pm
unremembered the detail edge past cutting
a photograph I didn't take of my mother as a girl in winter
to break up the rhythm if this is a diary or worthless

broken sleet, uncertain & solitary & even that
is wrong, the word wanted is *relinquish*
to be precise. Outlines can be enough
or haunting, nothing or everything / empty.

2.3.1.0

Cities of rooftops & streets bare trees against the lovely blueness of
   twilight.
FB says her daughter was born a few hours ago. A picture.
The neighbour's porch light on across the street.
The cat sleeping, dreaming under the desk lamp where it's warm.

"Shuttered with branches, dark in the afternoon."
Walls & bridges, heights & ruins or else choice redeemed.
What went wrong for which of us?
Why does the weather matter? A message arrives.

Your voice heard again in archived voice mail
can't call you back breathless & hopeful unbroken
at that beginning even if the fox knows gnawing on silences
learning not to ask or indirectly.

Alone. Without remembering or acting on memory.
Returning without memory this last time again.
At liberty. Before decision. In contemplation.
A pebble gathering speed only now again. 12:56 pm. Overcast.

2.3.1.1

Oath of stones & maple keys / bicycle bells / collapse
toward bright noise aphorism & error
can't call you back breathless & hopeful unbroken
by hand, time & weather the sky

a catenary arc is not a parabola it's weighted down.
Doesn't it drop away another red thread or prophecy another
difference between a secret & an apple tree,
neither a philosopher nor a war correspondent comfortable

tangle complication delight entrance a glass staircase & granite cut
    incision
tearing deeply away. Real embodied equivalence.
Eating an apple now.
When scattered or lost or noise or

that time cannot be applied to them —
the converse not necessarily
never & always only geometry not at a distance
books reread returned to for comfort or provocation make a London in
    the mind.

2.3.1.2

An action continuing in the present
that continuity the assumption taking up past
& future memory rewritten but not all
the rewriting replacing hours & hands, some empty—

Who would want to give this up?
The wind diaspora of answers geodesic
"from self & from things & from persons; & growing between them,
    indifference"
clocks fast / slow / in phase & slipping 2:48 am

always walking a shattered road of
small packages & precious improvisations
its order only
imposed by the desire for order another network

cold rain too the bare tree on Crawford Street
clearly visible fractal reach of its branches
as if the purpose of light in another city to
glimpse a fox in this civil twilight London say—

2.3.1.3

1:59 pm. Mostly cloudy for the hour. Every equation an approximation
that undoes itself falling like space or each repetition is not noise
beginning again or not if there is no end the beginning
that voice these voices & how that implicates not enough to
  continue—

Why the *Four Quartets* still? A faded star, part of a reactionary
constellation now. Eternity isn't much concern at this table & if
"history is now & England"
it's small & always far away. That war ended 70 years ago. That war.

The precarity of rubble without rhythm or self-similarity.
Places in the forest where bones surface 50 years after
the crime. Not here. Maybe a zipper pull. A rivet.
The gold nib of a fountain pen, ink-scaled

in a fractal mesh of maybe & conditional present
tense experienced not reasoned intuition that
the wave function collapses again & again in melancholy geometry's
many repetitions / highest apple / tree or fox—

2.3.2.0

In revision interrupt myself with memory.
War is not coincidence so.
Not chronologically ordered, not altered by the passage
only see it & only at times / darkly—

3:02 pm. Partly cloudy. Partly cloudy for the hour.
No constellations but the spiral turn of the hinged sky
is real or real enough cold of course the danger is
to fall into yourself & say nothing having felt nothing.

The century pivoted on certainty & the clockwork came undone.
Every shard its own trajectory, beyond ballistic falling free
"the future futureless, before the morning watch"
the illusion of isolation hides constant / interaction.

Briefly & just a page with its mechanisms & adornments
left over from coherent causal days patterned & directed
not unlike breathing. That's past. Ink. Time. Weather.
In the asthmatic present hard enough to anticipate the end of a line.

2.3.2.1

If you shatter into 1,000 (& one) stories
children playing in the street this afternoon
& singing (that's rare) in discordant concord
interrupted by reply & post arriving.

Time then unmetabolized imperfect betrayed by the fiction of precision
remembering clouds & no detail every clock
stopped the instant it comes into existence
only imagination & entirely present recall

7:23 pm. By heart or memory not belief
in this place in this time maybe only
nostalgia is possible that pain
all that's left of homecoming now.

"A symbol perfected in death"
only slant lines thin memory
& no shelter visible. Precise parallels in 2 directions
a mirror you could step through broken glass—

2.3.2.2

Kingfisher or killdeer in the distance.
As the falling clock slows we know incrementally
this happened then this happened
or leave pages blank nothing uncovered

moment grey outside now desk lamp & papers here writing
aureole, variable, wind again, warm skin.
If self falls apart in pebbles or bread crumbs—
FB says her daughter was born a few hours ago. A picture.

The clock counting frame by frame.
Breathless & hopeful unbroken distance. Forgetting & retelling.
Moonlight on blackout streets. Bodies & body parts. Erased.
Always beginning out of time a chalkboard to make notes on wipe away
    clouds

with sunrise moonrise now & then
as if you could choose to remember or forget
threads through scratches on this soft wood.
What was the weather like, the crossing?

2.3.2.3

"Having answered light to light & being silent, the light is still"
& splendour! it does NOT cohere the better for it a lifetime spent
trying to say what's missing / mountains / high clear sky / curtained dusk
all of it returning desolation, angelic order or stage direction / A country
road. A tree. / Evening.

"That we are sound, substantial, made of flesh & blood"
less & less let's say the frame shrinks around the clock
to an effective point lost information
that will survive the fall into infinitely compressed light—

"Setting forth & not returning."
Colour words without colour. Numbers without counting.
Place names without places. Unrecognized smiles.
No stories. A first memory perhaps not possible.

"The only hope or else despair"
in strange duty closing the door on ruins
of machinery again. 3:42 pm. Overcast. Identifying
Dürer's *Melencolia* with the angel of history—

2.3.3.0

The question of burial remains & if elegy
"is prayer, observance, discipline, thought & action"
but always another's words the beautiful
or the fox unexpected & subtle.

It wasn't like that. Ever. Steel & copper
wreckage piled up to make a mountain.
Forest growing up around the workshop.
Greyblue parallels edging light, incantation, weather—

the set of all points which can be reached
along integral curves from a given point
by the transformations generated by commuting vector fields
forming an immersed 2-dimensional submanifold.

5:34 pm. Light rain for the hour.
Time slips & to measure it each alone
the child neglected in overwhelming
or waking in an empty house valuing solitude.

2.3.3.1

That this is also love. That a utility van
a yellow green ladder trade name Featherlite
racked on its roof is parked across the street. Two orange pylons.
Cross that out, it's gone now.

Probabilities don't compel, are only useful when action is repeated.
Not determined even if determinism can be predictably complex
in its strange attractions. Some deeper brighter transience.
Nothing up my sleeve except now a lion. (That trick never works.)

7:23 pm. By heart or memory not belief
in this place in this time maybe only
nostalgia is possible that pain
all that's left of homecoming now.

I don't know if silence is written by hand
a drawerful of stainless-steel cubes some with fine threaded holes
also small brass shims disordered & slippery with light machine oil
"the complete consort dancing together."

2.3.3.2

"Having answered light to light & being silent, the light is still."
No abandoned country churches, worn-away gravestones, overgrown
    rosebushes.
Stubble after harvest & highlight of first snow.
The sound of an airliner climbing over the wind.

"That we are sound, substantial, made of flesh & blood"
like rain 5:28 pm unremembered the detail edge past cutting
a photograph I didn't take of my mother as a girl in winter
to break up the rhythm if this is a diary or worthless.

"Setting forth & not returning"
what tradition remains to be unfolded & reread
what value & answering the sleepers in the underground
blacked-out windows & the few walking dark streets.

"The only hope or else despair"
a single sheet, some red thread untangled unknotted not yet stitched.
The first street lights & stars almost purple sky.
To the mailbox at the end of the block. Gone. Walk home.

2.3.3.3

The neighbour's porch light on across the street.
What tradition remains to be unfolded & reread
evolves even with many documents destroyed paper
toward bright noise aphorism & error

flew off silent in the cool of the morning now
or the markers of immediate sensation —
writing water & rocks, not even that in winter.
An epiphany. How to answer that? With leaving.

There is no plan, just repetition. Another page.
It's all there. A hologram. Vulture Peak or the Paradiso.
Break up this rhythm
falling & disappear in the dry cold air sublimation

in the desert air remembered an object or words
a few children wondering at the clotted clouds.
Incredible colour
fixed uniquely by momentum.

& if I interrupt myself
again or for the twenty-sixth time
being in a room without windows, doors & then
there you are in the garden (almost winter garden) not
that you ever found the way out
but this is outside wind
& leaves. Not Jerome's room—

                                        & if I interrupt myself
                        again or for the twenty-seventh time
                                                again, here, now
                                          the thought that this
                                         angel is also terrifying
                despite history & the theory of it even
                              immanent experience all
                                          the monumental
                                          useless artwork
                            lifework bodywork & none
                          of it left now, these lines—

1

3.0.0.0

The *English Suites*? Calculations of the Riemann curvature tensor?
Different from the moment you're certain you're out of the woods across
   the frontier all clear
in another city of grey stones somewhat abstract.
What you want is explanation & at some time or point

marking time precisely or rough as sandpaper to smooth
convenient forgetting & unasked for
joy of it endless, embodiment.
There are still a few pages left.

Through uncertain windows even this comfort is no inside
of everything I do not have & cannot—
or coloured in bright tropic orange green or dark blue—
break up the rhythm if this is a diary or worthless

& how long it takes to remember nothing if forgetting matters.
Not even one cold full stop of feeling
coastline doubling back to television snow Orion.
Time. Weather. Every equation an approximation.

3.0.0.1

12:49 pm. Clear. Clear for the hour.
What you want is explanation & at some time or point
it's blown away & sure you could catch the torn page
paint on it what self-portrait tree skeleton grid—

if you are real or the children's voices
"& destitution of all property"
the whole sentimental tradition when we believed in time absolutely
hard to mark beginning exactly interrupting myself with again

not the same as coming to the end of it under Orion
throwing my keys off the bridge out onto the ice & walking away the
    damage
irreversible trajectory past & out falling further forward
sublime fragmented emptiness shards not even shards of the same thing

what state of mind now radiant
if self falls apart in pebbles or bread crumbs
an unravelling series a red thread beginning
the door on that maybe beginning—

3.0.0.2

The time doesn't matter as much now. Urgency has drained away.
Breathless & hopeful unbroken distance. Forgetting & retelling.
Every memory provisional. A kind of numbness or improvisation.
A line should go here echoing something else.

Some darker clouds, light rain today through Wednesday.
2:24 pm. Without philosophy, occupation, charge, beyond
temporal order & forgetting or disorder & error
that time cannot be applied to them—

"Something I have said before. I shall say it again."
Walls & bridges, heights & ruins or else choice redeemed.
What went wrong for which of us?
Why does the weather matter? A message arrives.

Some of the geometrical properties of a manifold
can be most easily examined by constructing a manifold
called a fibre bundle which is locally
the direct product of the manifold & a suitable space.

3.0.0.3

On the facing page sunlight edging through the blinds in bright triangles
could build any geometry intervals of affection repeated & different
sun & stars not points of light extended threads stitched through time
red thread / orange / terrible blue white now without now & no memory
  of it—

Now leaves dry & about to having
long enough ago thin between brittle dust or air
timestrewn & nightrisked unwrapped knotted entire or measure
the story set aside for another jewel green evasion—

Because of its generality, this theorem does not tell us
whether the singularity will be in our past or in the future of our past.
The foreign necessary & no prayer & not much art or scope
left behind unordered reflections turning into the abstract double helix of
  migraine—

12:34 pm. Clear. Clear for the hour.
At this old pine table quiet street slight wind
"the silent listening to the undeniable—"
at least I'll fill this page always one more thing.

3.0.1.0

And this is the centre of the century the pane of glass the rock
"driven on the wind that sweeps the gloomy hills of London"
silence not ending it still & fire not ending it & ashes not ending it
every language burnt & written on air hot metal & dust—

growing up among foreigners our native
speech an imposter unmarked by signs
watching closely what's expected & only once asking
what you knew. 10:23 pm. Clear for the hour.

No question of flame or purity, refined
inarticulate now
is prose isn't it? Sometimes
it's hard to tell what's leaving.

Why the *Four Quartets* still? A faded star, part of a reactionary
constellation now. Eternity isn't much concern at this table & if
books reread returned to for comfort or provocation make a London in
    the mind
it's small & always far away. That war ended 70 years ago. That war.

3.0.1.1

The ashes of stories memories of fire & the sound of fire
the same shape but similar enough to say the same forget the time entirely.
Small wind written by hand just disturbs
how to empty out the teaching.

Some dream of history, dreams of almost
revising light fall freely & unconstrained
clearly visible fractal reach of its branches
at your feet papers in the wind imagine one copy

under fading dust wrappers sky blue cloth fine with no markings or
    annotations to return to.
Time falls away or falls anyway geodesic
neither noise nor silence uncertain bright
torn up if I interrupt myself time & weather—

Read this now. That word. Zero. What do you think?
That man & his books, or that child & the games
no more to say a matter of hearsay
aureole, variable, wind again, warm skin.

3.0.1.2

Sit with my back to the tree leaning looking up
into the net of sky / not infinite / receding
having lost my way in connections but not connected
reminding myself that I can delete this rewrite substantially—

That this is also love. That a utility van
a yellow green ladder trade name Featherlite
"here between the hither & the farther shore—"
Cross that out, it's gone now.

Cloud of unknowing brief & always cloud
of forgetting that cloud shaped like
a continent a coastline foam left
by waves breaking before the next wave knowing

at this table scraps of the 20th century measured out
in more than one book not to be reconciled the book closed for the
moment grey outside 3:36 pm desk lamp & papers here writing
in black ink borrowed authority to replace feeling with—

3.0.1.3

There are comets in our lifetime.
The speaking subject cannot be so easily
aureole, variable, wind again, warm skin.
Sound of the river below unseeded. Not winter.

Break up this rhythm.
Elliptical, allusive vague light
ends the aftermath a wound & not a new idea
exists without you.

Falling because falling is so complex it's simple [geodesic equation]
a fading tangle of loops & thread red thread & dried-up dark purple
again as if again memory is fallible who knew
a place we can walk through a house or a neighbourhood—

Briefly & just a page with its mechanisms & adornments
left over from coherent causal days patterned & directed
"setting forth & not returning"
not unlike breathing. That's past. Ink. 6:31 pm. Partly cloudy.

3.0.2.0

2:12 pm. Clear. Clear for the hour. The time before.
Fire only breathes in & ascends. Chemical fire.
Not an element. Every differentiable symmetry
of the action has a corresponding conservation law.

The background changes (cat on the piano, empty coffee cup)
half full of wanting to or having wanted now learning maybe
here alone those moments it curls up tight coherent causal
I think Tom just perhaps but that passes.

Refusal & execution
a single sheet & some red thread
heavily enjambed middle now time.
Some truth in painting.

Starting to the rain slowing back to polyrhythms
"like the past, to have no destination"
small sparks you keep finding for weeks.
Broken concrete. Warm wood.

3.0.2.1

Predicted is that beautiful or ornament
"the murmuring shell of time, & not in any language"
proof that zero is always & everywhere that time
1:38 pm. Clear for the hour.

Time. Weather. Every equation an approximation
that undoes itself falling like space or each repetition is not noise
beginning again or not if there is no end the beginning
that voice these voices & how that implicates not enough to continue—

I keep losing the thread red thread that felt like falling again
only natural nothing pushing back not even a clock an event
of some significance like a wheelbarrow or the internet hold it in your
hand it scampers off just grey enough

without wires gears ailerons condensers just grey & some vibration
which is different from the bees in the purple sage scent
in the desert air remembered an object or words
or wheels a sort of useless machine counting cannot be a poem.

3.0.2.2

Wind bending the trees in the east burning information.
Early, waking before dawn, walking.
Mechanical time. This then that. The stem
of the windowed room is empty the windows are empty

snow fills the air this way then that way & the way
in the fog in a place you don't know.
Lines crossed out.
Time. Weather. A key turning. Plain text. A door.

Some are detained at the border & will not pass.
Do I refuse recollection or is there nothing to remember?
The description of a scent or taste or touch
convenient forgetting & unasked for

small tonal transitions of the black & white past
neither a philosopher nor a war correspondent comfortable.
If you move & there are ruins & ruins
for hours the world almost—

3.0.2.3

All is not lost. To wonder what grace this leaves us with
what tradition remains to be unfolded & reread
what value & answering the sleepers in the underground
blacked-out windows & the few walking dark streets

after the ordinary dinner (bread, wine, apples) a few
words some kind most disinterested the wind unquestioning
"ardour & selflessness & self-surrender"
& a song even if every note is melancholia or a number

the set of all points which can be reached
along integral curves from a given point
by the transformations generated by commuting vector fields
forming an immersed 2-dimensional submanifold.

11:04 am. Mostly cloudy. Light rain starting in 15 minutes
so nothing begins because the breath
is held, the body is held, tension in the calves & shoulders
no thought no thought no thought—

3.0.3.0

Always falling wind before the firestorms adding up histories.
Wind bending the trees in the east burning information.
Did she follow the fox or the lightening says nothing.
Stopped clock. Shadow hands broken face. Ash-sweet night.

There is no plan, just repetition. Another page.
"The silent withering of autumn flowers."
Any beginning breaks the smooth surface &
recollection returns, breathing becomes difficult again, wearying

& the comfort of banality more tempting not fire
not concerned not looking at old photographs or letters or emails
for answers if noise is indistinguishable
good as reading great books copying lines down from the radio who has a
    radio—

3:08 pm. Partly cloudy. Partly cloudy for the hour.
There are some true things or things thought to be true
& so shrines are built outside cause & effect.
It's all there. A hologram. Vulture Peak or the Paradiso.

3.0.3.1

Time. By heart or memory not belief
in this place in this time maybe only
nostalgia is possible that pain
all that's left of homecoming now.

Voices from the street not my language. The thrush again. Sparrows.
The quiet is important why is the quiet important.
Answering. Not a sound. Listen higher everywhere
tinnitus of the quantum vacuum massed choir —

10:25 am. Overcast. A key turning. Plain text. A door.
It's difficult to touch this exactly being erased
"setting forth & not returning"
I thought I saw something in your eyes.

Probabilities don't compel, are only useful when action is repeated.
Not determined even if determinism can be predictably complex
in its strange attractions. Some deeper brighter transience.
Nothing up my sleeve except now a lion. (That trick never works.)

3.0.3.2

If this is never spoken of if this didn't happen.
If matter curves space & space tells matter how to move.
If you move & there are ruins & ruins.
"If our temporal reversion nourish—"

6:28 pm. Mostly cloudy. Rain beginning in the hour.
Walls & bridges, heights & ruins or else choice redeemed.
What went wrong for which of us?
Why does the weather matter? A message arrives

& this is the centre of the century the pane of glass the rock
hurled at the lightening cracks radiating before the slivers crash
silence not ending it still & fire not ending it & ashes not ending it
every language burnt & written on air hot metal & dust—

Unsure of this like light the rain doesn't have edges either
adrift maybe wishing time away & night to come
direct, simple, a gift after a lot of labour that time actually
measures something. Quickly. Again. Quickly.

3.0.3.3

Only begin & begin again & what's left after
this is the centre of the century the pane of glass the rock
different from the moment you're certain you're out of the woods. Across
    the frontier all clear
on Crawford I see from my window writing is a maple of course

in anything like language the place shatters
desire exploding that calm symmetry massing is it regret—
or Kensington or Copenhagen, encrypted dark
& singing (that's rare) in discordant concord.

The explanatory entropy on the wall
so nothing begins because the breath
not the same as memory or a book or a wristwatch.
But there's no anger because anger is death that's right

being able to take back what is not said & a whole literature
only slant lines thin memory
of a library of wolves fresh cave fox shadows—
not the act itself or alone.

& if I interrupt myself
again or for the twenty-eighth time
enough to end there
say a bell with a rope
pull
tied off somewhere to the right out
of the frame
but now put your tools down again
without rage, impatience &c
deserving respect—

& if I interrupt myself
again or for the twenty-ninth time
obviously unfinished, provisional
as it was always going to be
a few fragments retrieved from
what?
No one to answer that.
No one to ask.
Telling myself once—
but memory is doubtful
unreliable &
I—

12

3.1.0.0

Tone of voice but not words
verify the one & disprove the other.
This is the centre of the century the pane of glass the rock
now reduces to the calculation of connection one-forms

the noise of accidents
for what light could say falling.
A small plane passes over. Perhaps the thrush again but that's not so.
Distance scattering error quantum error &

as the falling clock slows we know incrementally
in thoughts that are not treasures at all
& what could be known raw material
apples again, sliced up now, angle of each cut

but always another's words the beautiful
& it was autumn & there was a kingfisher —
Forget. These aren't your memories anyway.
Into the net of sky / not infinite / receding.

3.1.0.1

The existence of an apparent horizon
implies a component of the event horizon
outside it or coinciding
the converse not necessarily

12:57 pm. Clear. Clear for the hour.
Quickly. Tell repeatedly nothing at all nothing
in this quiet room not shoreline no waves
breaking the empty street the window still closed.

Questions themselves painful not thinking
in strange duty closing the door on ruins
of machinery again. Time & weather. Identifying
Dürer's *Melencolia* with the angel of history

as if action were enough. What do you do after that, & after after?
Live alone with your line breaks? Paperweights? Apples? That fox?
The *English Suites*? Calculations of the Riemann curvature tensor?
"Scolding, mocking, or merely chattering?"

3.1.0.2

In the diagonal rain perhaps a stranger
a slash of red at the cuff of a black sleeve the street
starting to the rain slowing back to polyrhythms
no one following memory rewritten pools at the curb where there should
    be reflections—

The passage work & so much left
undone unlived self shattering into myriad
bright prism points all across the floor
"but a lifetime burning in every moment"

so a list of losses at canonical hours (11:16 am. Mostly cloudy.)
in unusual coordinates an artifact of viewpoint centrifugal
love & strife or is it love & disease or theft & early transcendentals.
No beginning is the highest truth I've heard.

How time stops for some the moment of triumph or terror
emotion tangled up in cool not colour / scatter
a measure of the unpredictability of information content
& so a theory of surprise. Not time or dreams.

3.1.0.3

If this is never spoken of if this didn't happen.
If matter curves space & space tells matter how to move.
If you move & there are ruins & ruins.
If I interrupt myself—

Do I refuse recollection or is there nothing to remember?
A thrush was singing but it's quiet now.
Far-off construction. A power saw.
Then an airliner, & a car horn.

11:26 am. Mostly cloudy for the hour.
Starting to the rain slowing back to polyrhythms
small sparks you keep finding for weeks.
Broken concrete. Warm wood.

"Setting forth & not returning"
turn the page. Memory is fire in its cabinet
fire without light or heat dark & pure burning.
The book will sag & melt, a dull pool & no stars.

3.1.1.0

Unreliable time in a froth of emptiness
& what could be known raw materials
"decay with imprecision, will not stay in place"
long since rebuilt in the modern style

thinking they matter or they don't, taking refuge
in thoughts that are not treasures at all
repeating empty hands & an empty glass
where to end the line the stanza or page.

4:28 pm. Overcast. Overcast for the hour.
Only pure grey bones left unburied ash of stars just stars & all the dark
    between
a story we could make up
tired of paper tangled minds & scraps I believed that once—

Not being able to say what is forgotten or not remembered not
being able to take back what is not said & a whole literature
of conversion belief modernism even if it was a literature
of shards the bombed-out shell of the cathedral random light—

3.1.1.1

Who lives there now? A character from an old book,
tangle complication delight entrance a glass staircase &
lovely lists of the names of flowers
oil paint meaning for example there

is wrong, the word wanted is *relinquish*.
The problem that words mean something.
Freedom or loss? Without edges or scatters
this unopened book set aside & from memory

a pebble gathering speed only now again. Time. Weather.
Any beginning breaks the smooth surface &
another city in which strangers throng & buy
sees this physics in action.

Then an airliner, & a car horn
without clocks how small time is church bells & canonical hours.
Doesn't it drop away another red thread or prophecy another
measurement & perspective exception & rule I can't speak to.

3.1.1.2

"To set a crown upon your lifetime's effort"
a drawerful of stainless-steel cubes some with fine threaded holes
also small brass shims disordered & slippery with light machine oil
aphorism & scale independent error silences differ.

Now leaves dry & about to having
long enough ago thin between brittle dust or air
timestrewn & nightrisked unwrapped knotted entire or measure
the story set aside for another jewel green evasion.

I stopped listening
built a low wall between the house & the street under the pines
dividing the living from the dead, like snow.
7:23 pm. Light rain stopping in 25 minutes.

No whole these are parts of.
Void scattered & complex.
The long century broken into sentences or just broken
shaking off the night coming in from the rain morning.

3.1.1.3

"The only hope or else despair"
 of the broken glass at the roadside
 the detailed cross-hatching read as texture
 not noise or a diamond cutting through

5:34 pm. Light rain for the hour.
 Time slips & to measure it each alone
 the child neglected in overwhelming
 or waking in an empty house valuing solitude.

Even when names remain who is there to say
 that man & his books, or that child & the games
 she played, chalk on sidewalk, Himmel oder Hölle, Angry Birds—
 Forget. These aren't your memories anyway.

I keep losing the thread red thread that felt like falling again
 only natural nothing pushing back not even a clock an event
 of some significance like a wheelbarrow or the internet hold it in your
 hand it scampers off just grey enough—

3.1.2.0

By geometry & the allegory of the Riemann curvature tensor
all in elegy preceded rewritten read
some left out after all those missing
"trying to learn to use words, & every attempt"

vicious slices & shards all edges
small sparks you keep finding for weeks
again & again every diamond cut into—
4:41 pm. Clear. Clear for the hour.

The passage work & so much left
undone unlived self shattering into myriad
bright prism points all across the floor
at your feet papers in the wind imagine one copy.

The beginning is delight again.
Joy of it endless, embodiment
pure & outside time, & the memory
of joy is not joy but can perhaps—

3.1.2.1

Sans brilliant vision in sunlight morning
without skill or apology the wind & building breathing
"both intimate & unidentifiable"
fragments & suspicion sometimes an insincere act.

12:08 pm. Overcast. Reliable quiet after rain
cool spring & a few early flowers
iris reticulata blue as the beginning
of night & yellow crocus uncomplicated

the present not a moment but a duration not a neighbourhood
but this room depending how you got here & where you started when
did you decide to leave the vines covered the old factories red
& is the past an object polyhedron or smooth curves differentiable—

In the diagonal rain perhaps a stranger
a slash of red at the cuff of a black sleeve the street
starting to the rain slowing back to polyrhythms
no one following memory rewritten pools at the curb where there should
    be reflections—

3.1.2.2

From geometry & falling or falling, drawing
as a function of proper time measured on,
to come or being lived through
constellation now. Eternity isn't much concern at this table & if

mark time along each one. Learn to draw like that
shaking off the night coming in from the rain morning.
Time. By heart or memory not belief
the illusion of isolation hides constant / interaction.

Missing rhythm of absence or silence punctuated vacuum.
Not there can't vanish it does
scampers off just grey enough
to preserve, to elevate, to cancel.

It's hard to tell what's leaving.
How often again looking at them & looking
is wrong, the word wanted is *relinquish*
unlike bones or metal insignia of rank.

3.1.2.3

Of branching light & dark displaced covariant derivatives
life burnt away radiant life & no ash of words
on broken glass gravestones, thorn bushes growing.
2:38 pm. Partly cloudy for the hour.

Despite the constrained perspective & the lectern & the lion & the pen
the windowed room is empty the windows are empty
the scratching on the paper empty which is different than erased
which I have heard & still the lion growls or purrs in his radiant sleep

thinking they matter or they don't, taking refuge
in thoughts that are not treasures at all
repeating empty hands & an empty glass
where to end the line the stanza or page.

Impossible to see time
"& know the place for the first time."
Only trees threading light netted by the wind.
What wasn't found.

3.1.3.0

As if you could choose to remember or forget
ask what has been left interruption
lovely lists of the names of flowers—
2:33 pm. Overcast for the hour.

Between deaths & gestures objects as raw as prayer
is impossible even the memory of prayer
a skinny dog sleeping by the millstone & the workshop's tumble
measurement & perspective exception & rule I can't speak to—

Who would want to give this up?
The wind diaspora of answers geodesic
never void & always void
clocks fast / slow / in phase & slipping time

"setting forth & not returning"
here not present but present
this far away it's almost Euclidean
contradiction that is real feeling.

3.1.3.1

Where you can stand in the middle
time conjectured, unremembered, walk
or look down at the froth & flow, imagine
writing water & rocks, not even that in winter.

OK, self shatters & the shards are dangerous still
interrupted by hawk migration in cloudless sky the self presented
    here &
interrupted by never getting past half empty now
the selves lived, stains on a shirt you thought was clean

as if you could choose to remember or forget
ask what has been left interruption
lovely lists of the names of flowers
"the only hope or else despair—"

12:57 pm. Clear. Clear for the hour.
No site or formal counterpoint no machine of time
variation & associative logic beyond constraint
the same & not the same a path of scatters—

3.1.3.2

The question of burial remains & if elegy
or something black can't say another word
but always another's words the beautiful
or the fox unexpected & subtle

in a fractal mesh of maybe & conditional present
tense experienced not reasoned intuition that
the wave function collapses again & again in melancholy geometry
"& the children in the apple tree—"

An action continuing in the present
that continuity the assumption taking up past
& future memory rewritten but not all
the rewriting replacing hours & hands, some empty—

Unsure of this like light the rain doesn't have edges either
adrift maybe wishing time away & night to come
direct, simple, a gift after a lot of labour that time actually
measures something. 2:43 pm. Light rain.

3.1.3.3

Remember. A small dog barking at the garbage collectors.
Sometimes a black white light radiance.
No ticket stubs or pocket journal datebooks or cups full of coloured pencils
    & war poetry or volumes of the Stockholm edition of the works of
    Thomas Mann.
Not the act itself or alone.

A love letter & bibliography, geometry, the fox at the roadside
of life. Rewriting the same pages.
A country road. A tree. Evening.
Nevertheless despite these limitations one can still predict

broken afterwards shell pits filled with rain or groundwater.
The clock counting frame by frame.
Repeated small pieces even if self-correcting
threads through scratches on this soft wood

oath of stones & maple keys / bicycle bells / collapse —
never & always only geometry not at a distance
grey galvanized past ringing details —
no wristwatches stopped at random times.

& if I interrupt myself
again or for the thirtieth time
for now
even if (say it!) it
will never be. Awkward
to admit you aren't getting it.
You? At this table again as
twilight thickens, more lines
scratched by hand, wrong again:
they flow—

& if I interrupt myself
again or for the thirty-first time
or has it been longer, much longer,
& did that first war ever end or echo
into all the others, forward & back, past
as you have it 2 lines later writing
of a different matter—

8

3.2.0.0

The story is not the life / remembered
next a master clock
all that's left of homecoming now.
By hand, imperfect concentration but applying it directly,

an essay of shards & swerves, strange attractors
without clocks how small time is church bells & canonical hours.
Cross that out, it's gone now.
It doesn't have to make sense like a welder or

experimental tests of general relativity
& splendour! it does NOT cohere the better for it a lifetime spent
not even one cold full stop of feeling
temporal order & forgetting or disorder & error

that voice these voices & how that implicates not enough to
    continue—
The soft comfort of small hunger
action conditioned & dependent still life.
Light shifts. Light slants, conciliate or another word.

3.2.0.1

It wasn't much. A bird speaking. A thrush
kingfisher or killdeer in the distance.
I wrote letters that were answered.
We spoke for hours. We still see each other sometimes.

It doesn't have to make sense like a welder
or Kensington or Copenhagen, encrypted dark
matter implied by its effect on observables
"old fires to ashes, & ashes to the earth."

At a certain point in time the cost of memory
exceeds the cost of never knowing & everything—dishes, scissors,
    perfume bottles, shoe racks, magazines, Chinese rugs, salt, luggage,
    silhouettes, leaf rake,
the I don't know & that's the point—
2:22 pm. Rain stopping. Subtle edges of fast clouds.

To acknowledge nothing there or not much still writing
imagined light tracking abstract across white walls
how much hope doesn't matter. A crystal palace collapsing
sun on glass siren distance no longer simply connected.

3.2.0.2

Perhaps forgetting is pure unknowing possible
understanding something of it as it comes apart.
"Between midnight & dawn, when the past is all deception"
clock time in silence / no return / one way

no whole these are parts of.
Void scattered & complex.
The long century broken into sentences or just broken
shaking off the night coming in from the rain morning.

No more bright punctuation or shiny word-coins.
Small breakfasts, sometimes in the garden. 7:16 am.
Call it a garden. Like the description of a flower
the description of a scent or taste or touch.

Time then unmetabolized imperfect betrayed by the fiction of precision
remembering clouds & no detail every clock
stopped the instant it comes into existence
only imagination & entirely present recall.

3.2.0.3

Hollowing loss empty as feeling & always
repeat myself & interrupt myself
because there's no end to it & is that supposed to be a comfort?
There was a kingfisher. That's all.

Complex hierarchies fall away jewel by jewel
thought, intent, grace, silence, mind, truth,
"moment, the moment in & out of time,"
dispossessed, abstract & unbodied the way mathematics is—

Spatter, leopard, the starry sky or smallpox scar
& writing by hand living inside this
eating an apple 3:16 pm sunny
a roomful of light / a door.

To acknowledge nothing there or not much still writing
imagined light tracking abstract across white walls
how much hope doesn't matter. A crystal palace collapsing
sun on glass siren distance no longer simply connected.

3.2.1.0

Voices from the street not my language. The thrush again. Sparrows.
"The dahlias sleep in the empty silence."
Answering. Not a sound. Listen higher everywhere
tinnitus of the quantum vacuum massed choir—

The present not a moment but a duration not a neighbourhood
but this room depending how you got here & where you started when
did you decide to leave the vines covered the old factories red
& is the past an object polyhedron or smooth curves differentiable—

No wristwatches stopped at 8:15 am with cloud cover less than ³⁄₁₀th
    at all altitudes
no brown paper & twine & wrapping paper
no photocopies of prints by Dürer vacation postcards or beach stones
no ticket stubs or pocket journal datebooks or cups full of coloured pencils
    & war poetry or volumes of the Stockholm edition of the works of
    Thomas Mann.

This is the centre of the century the pane of glass the rock
hurled at the lightening cracks radiating before the slivers crash
silence not ending it still & fire not ending it & ashes not ending it
every language burnt & written on air hot metal & dust—

3.2.1.1

Throwing my keys off the bridge out onto the ice & walking away the
    damage
the feel & smell of an old book not death held open in 2 hands & for
    example on page 68 or 289 or 380 or 387 or 432
measurement & perspective exception & rule I can't speak to.
On the facing page sunlight edging through the blinds in bright triangles

constellation now. Eternity isn't much concern at this table & if
tinnitus of the quantum vacuum massed choir—
lines crossed out.
No question of flame or purity, refined

theorems on singularities
held, the body is held, tension in the calves & shoulders.
Maybe an excess. Maybe better to say
slightly different & a small change in flavour

out of time the fabric of belief.
Filling a family of curves
the delusion of black & white
to come or being lived through.

3.2.1.2

In a fractal mesh of maybe & conditional present
tense experienced not reasoned intuition that
the wave function collapses again & again in melancholy geometry's
many repetitions / highest apple / tree or fox—

not contradiction a salamander in the fire or at your feet at the threshold
quick motion all corners in this cottage or gentrified row house
the trees filling in the light more patterned sidewalk & quiet I get
  distracted.
2:21 pm. Clear. Clear for the hour.

All they'll say decades later beginning partway down
a lifetime & still walking time & weather
unrecalled green leaves maybe no coat yet
"if I think, again, of this place"

present moment stretching if
there are no flowers & there
are not understandings that
faint edge memory just a few words—

3.2.1.3

Not being able to say what is forgotten or not remembered not
being able to take back what is not said & a whole literature
of conversion belief modernism even if it was a literature
of shards the bombed-out shell of the cathedral random light—

slow anniversaries mark the fixed frame
of life. Rewriting the same pages.
Not meaning but morning that fails
& fails again, no better for being / repeated

emptiness itself & wind & forgetting possibly
a distant siren fire trash collection 9:17 am snow
remembering ash cans made of metal
grey galvanized past ringing details—

"a condition of complete simplicity"
& perhaps in error & not empty not pure
sit & turn it over & over in your otherwise
empty hands never done with—

3.2.2.0

It wasn't much. A bird speaking. A thrush
kingfisher or killdeer in the distance.
I wrote letters that were answered
"under the oppression of the silent fog."

Watch each thought's trajectory through time as memory ravels round
    itself
always in the present tense. No going back. The house anticipated at the
    end
of the lane warm lit windows in the twilight woods torn clouds thin moon.
Who lives there now? A character from an old book.

Or buy old watches disassemble them & determine by practical
    observation
what colour their ashes are & if digital ashes differ from analog
& how long it takes to remember nothing if forgetting matters.
4:10 pm. Mostly cloudy. Light snow starting in 6 minutes.

Then it curves & falls back to absence
all the old thoughts or just a thread
caught on something like an improvisation
out of time the fabric of belief.

3.2.2.1

Impossible to see time
only trees threading light netted by the wind.
What wasn't found.
"Accept the constitution of silence."

Dreaming a different garden, shady, an oak & an owl
flew off silent in the cool of the morning 6:55 am
dead raven & carrion bird in the grass. Flies.
The unkempt awkward folding flap of wings after they land.

No hope to recall only hope to fall through & at some time
all shall be well enough not that I believe any such thing only
the approximate curve of the geodesic equations subject to quantum
    corrections
I don't know any way to calculate being comforted by incompletion.

When scattered or lost or noise or
falling turbulence not an atlas not
directions not a guide not definitive
not coherent except by accident—

3.2.2.2

Still down your tools compass square green mechanical
being able to take back what is not said & a whole literature
without philosophy, occupation, charge, beyond
that time cannot be applied to them—

marking time precisely or rough as sandpaper to smooth
read astronomy answer questions with evasion anything like truth.
Walls & bridges, heights & ruins or else choice redeemed.
A distant siren fire trash collection.

Did she follow the fox or the lightening says nothing
anyway looking at them
red thread / orange / terrible blue white now without now & no memory
    of it—
sight. Like that. Or even a waterglass.

Apples again, sliced up now, angle of each cut
not meaning but morning that fails
the present not a moment but a duration not a neighbourhood.
It's all there. A hologram. Vulture Peak or the Paradiso.

3.2.2.3

"Having answered light to light & being silent, the light is still,"
timepieces stopped broken willow shadows
washed by rain 10:57 pm & turbulence all
or some of the intermittencies of now revised—

On the facing page sunlight edging through the blinds in bright triangles
could build any geometry intervals of affection repeated & different
sun & stars not points of light extended threads stitched through time
"that we are sound, substantial, made of flesh & blood—"

"Setting forth & not returning"
time slips & to measure it each alone
the child neglected in overwhelming
or waking in an empty house valuing solitude.

Walk in the cold clear air & not
wear a watch or think about the time
what to do later today or tomorrow
"the only hope or else despair."

3.2.3.0

Here at the table writing by hand & rewriting by memory a few phrases
like time caught in the cloud chamber's physical trace
obsolete beautiful loops & spirals of charge & condensation
like writing by hand but nobody's hand no the hand of electricity—

12:34 pm. Clear. Clear for the hour.
At this old pine table quiet street slight wind
from the north slight turning of the leaves knowing
at least I'll fill this page always one more thing

"the wild thyme unseen, or the winter lightening"
old loves & current to address, letters, on paper
real & all of it properly radiant life / beautiful desire / gift
of everything I do not have & cannot—

What's hidden might stay an aphorism like the question of self
threads through scratches on this soft wood
geodesic grain & ashes of words mainly numbers
confused by speculation sentences I never got to—

3.2.3.1

Unacknowledged experience unspoken for
resists narrative to leave breathing in & breathing out
3:50 pm sunset at 4:51 pm overcast for the next hour
& rain this evening full moon above the clouds.

What state of mind now radiant
if self falls apart in pebbles or bread crumbs
an unravelling series a red thread beginning
the door on that maybe beginning—

It felt good to close the door
safe as houses
let daily life get on without looking.
Early, waking before dawn, walking

wet streets after rain meeting no one
look in all the usual places, prose now,
the delusion of black & white.
"Every poem an epitaph."

3.2.3.2

"Having answered light to light & being silent, the light is still"
as if it could all burn away with no question of pure ashes
the trajectory & distribution having no unique source tree
without roots or rooted in a cloud of unknowing only now

"that we are sound, substantial, made of flesh & blood"
there are too many sheets of paper not
infinite but another sense the wind takes them & the rain
puts them down without words. 1:19 pm. Whispering.

Falling because falling is so complex it's simple [geodesic equation]
a fading tangle of loops & thread red thread & dried-up dark purple
again as if again memory is fallible who knew
"setting forth & not returning."

The century pivoted on certainty & the clockwork came undone.
Every shard its own trajectory, beyond ballistic falling free
the illusion of isolation hides constant / interaction
"the only hope or else despair."

3.2.3.3

Breathing porcelain & asbestos
chance falling together
by hand, imperfect concentration but applying it directly
to another time or the sky / the escapement

from memory not life / by heart—
Unrecalled therefore unrepeated. Unnumbered. One one one.
Threads through scratches on this soft wood
No whole these are parts of.

Into stories when there are no stories
to say nothing, feel nothing, remember nothing, think
fire without light or heat dark & pure burning.
Forget. These aren't your memories anyway.

Read astronomy answer questions with evasion anything like truth.
There are no flowers & there
undone unlived self shattering into myriad
not fire but its deep blue core.

& if I interrupt myself
again or for the thirty-second time
there are 34 words missing—

& if I interrupt myself
again or for the thirty-third time
& if the numbers meant
there was use in them
rows columns & diagonals
summed to significance
decrepit so-called science
stranding us in Beauty.
Plain to see.
No predictive value
outside the frame of chance—

13

3.3.0.0

Rain this evening full moon above the clouds
& so a theory of surprise. Not time or dreams.
The book should not have page numbers.
OK, self shatters & the shards are dangerous still

the unkempt awkward folding flap of wings after they land
just grey enough
where to end the line the stanza / page
thought, intent, grace, silence, mind, truth.

Toward glorious luminary night & our early evening city
hard to mark beginning exactly interrupting myself with again
glimpse a fox in this civil twilight London say
the time after.

Not about memory or every
asthmatic present hard enough to anticipate the end of a line
or wheels a sort of useless machine counting cannot be a poem,
form an immersed 2-dimensional submanifold.

3.3.0.1

Or some of the intermittencies of now revised
I don't know any way to calculate being comforted by incompletion,
sun on glass siren distance no longer simply connected,
the whole sentimental tradition when we believed in time absolutely.

The speaking subject cannot be so easily
haunting, nothing or everything / empty
lines crossed out.
It wasn't like that. Ever. Steel & copper

anchoring quiet it's possible to touch,
to come or being lived through,
to consider loss when there was nothing.
These & most other instances of the propagation of light

as if action were enough. What do you do after that, & after after?
In its strange attractions some deeper brighter transience
of the lane warm lit windows in the twilight woods torn clouds thin moon.
Repeated small pieces even if self-correcting—

3.3.0.2

Geodesics that could have been or will have been if
to the mark chalk or ash or plumb line blue,
light as fast as possible the ruin of time.
How time stops for some the moment of triumph or terror

the soft comfort of small hunger
for example instead of a photograph.
No tongues of flame. A small envelope containing
waves breaking before the next wave knowing

another recollection or expectation questions.
Is it enough or more than enough
if you move & there are ruins & ruins
curving / falling / recited / absence.

The difficulty of knowing data on the whole of a spacelike surface,
the rewriting replacing hours & hands, some empty
anyway looking at them
all-pervasive, any past-directed timelike geodesic.

3.3.0.3

This close to the end come back to it
again & again every diamond cut into
what you knew. Now & weather.
No site or formal counterpoint no machine of time

when what are ashes or remembered
faint edge memory just a few words
neither a philosopher nor a war correspondent comfortable
argument or conspiracy, perhaps endearments, seduction—

Hold fast.
Sun & stars not points of light extended threads stitched through time
many repetitions / highest apple / tree or fox—
therefore inadequate covenant of

heavily enjambed middle now time.
Tired of paper tangled minds & scraps I believed that once.
Bright prism points all across the floor.
At liberty. Before decision. In contemplation.

3.3.1.0

More difficult than coming through nothing
exists without you.
At a certain point in time the cost of memory
not the same as coming to the end of it under Orion

the smell of death unforgettable revolting sweetness
whether the singularity will be in our past or in the future of our past.
Aphorism & scale independent error silences differ
the noise of accidents

deliberating & there is no refusal. Time & weather
dispossessed, abstract & unbodied the way mathematics is.
Devote yourself to calculation, enumeration,
a book beginning this & ending time, or burnt & one.

Frequencies of froth & foam the result of runoff from farm fields
children playing in the street this afternoon
eating an apple now
sharp edges, diffuse shadows, breathing.

3.3.1.1

Sound of the river below unseeded. Not winter.
Empty hands never done with
evolution even with many documents destroyed paper
a place we can walk through a house or a neighbourhood —

emotion tangled up in cool not colour / scatter
leaf green plates on the table left outside
flattening event & memory, error,
that man & his books, or that child & the games

we did that magnifying glass well mainly the corners
without memory rust or other words
in the past as territories measure.
Complex hierarchies fall away jewel by jewel

accumulation over years & unsymmetric silence
books reread returned to for comfort or provocation make a London in
    the mind
interrupted by reply & post arriving
barren ground of memory language scraped away.

3.3.1.2

An imaginary door or the letters that spell a door like memory
or leave pages blank nothing uncovered
clock time in silence / no return / one way
a distant siren fire trash collection

& it was autumn & there was a kingfisher—
repeating empty hands & an empty glass
& the small change in flavour, a sharper maybe, iron
when I was just winter streets

alone. Without remembering or acting on memory.
Time. Sunlight through leaves & shadows.
If I interrupt myself—
Jerome at his translations, a drafty room in Nuremberg.

Turn the page. Memory is fire in its cabinet.
Despite the constrained perspective & the lectern & the lion & the pen
to be 3-dimensional in the Schwarzschild coordinate system.
Broken concrete. Warm wood.

3.3.1.3

Without wires gears ailerons condensers just grey & some vibration
slush browngrey or cardboard.
All shall be well enough not that I believe any such thing only
something needs to interrupt me now.

Like an apple to set the time by reference
fields which obey well-behaved hyperbolic equations.
Did she follow the fox or the lightening says nothing
calculable if not predictable metaphor

the memory of touch not touch still the memory of memory
paper blown across the tabletop or shadows.
This is the centre of the century the pane of glass the rock
midday unopened books unfinished doubt

pools of rain & mossy stones, colder, wetter days getting shorter.
It felt good to close the door.
I stopped listening
line by line or cell by cell knowing what you know.

3.3.2.0

Slightly different & a small change in flavour
of familiar lines recalled & copying them out
a convenient name for the vector
a lifetime & still walking time & weather

& how long it takes to remember nothing if forgetting matters.
As objects end as objects
craters merging on the coast of ruins the rain pooling there
falling turbulence not an atlas not

unreliable celebration a future almost reconciled.
Then an airliner, & a car horn,
this unopened book set aside & from memory
or by hand it scampers off just grey enough.

Early winters almost remembered not exactly
a snowball thrown into the Grand Canyon by an 8-year-old.
Watch each thought's trajectory through time as memory ravels round
    itself
& perhaps in error & not empty not pure—

3.3.2.1

Having lost my way in connections but not connected
sharp edges, diffuse shadows, breathing
shadows may not be leaves
that will survive the fall into infinitely compressed light—

one voice or many, one then many
I know still. Left of the day
for answers if noise is indistinguishable
shards the bombed-out shell of the cathedral random light—

no ticket stubs or pocket journal datebooks or cups full of coloured pencils
   & war poetry or volumes of the Stockholm edition of the works of
   Thomas Mann—
There is anger. There is a war. A tearing. A dislocation
of the precise colour of time deeper
how it becomes cliché or stuck not dissolving

measurement & perspective exception & rule I can't speak to.
Sound of the river below unseeded. Not winter.
Taking as a text the Principle of Equivalence.
Who would want to give this up?

3.3.2.2

Small sparks you keep finding for weeks
the trajectory & distribution having no unique source tree.
Cloud of unknowing brief & always cloud
along integral curves from a given point.

The crack in the glass is part of it & the shadow
not unlike breathing. That's past. Ink. Time. Weather.
A love letter & bibliography, geometry, the fox at the roadside
in another city of grey stones somewhat abstract

the trees filling in the light more patterned sidewalk & quiet I get
    distracted.
Pure & outside time, & the memory
& rain if remembering stained radio noise.
I stopped listening.

Not contradiction a salamander in the fire or at your feet at the threshold
to another time or the sky / the escapement
& the small change in flavour, a sharper maybe, iron.
I don't know any way to calculate being comforted by incompletion.

3.3.2.3

The precarity of rubble without rhythm or self-similarity,
a skinny dog sleeping by the millstone & the workshop's tumble
less & less let's say the frame shrinks around the clock
not fire but its deep blue core.

Warm lit windows in the twilight woods torn clouds thin moon.
The passage work & so much left.
There's nothing special about these words,
the typography of the past repeated

list of is that beautiful or symbolic the rose garden voices
& how long it takes to remember nothing if forgetting matters.
It wasn't much. A bird speaking. A thrush
relationship between exterior derivatives

usually spatially separated can time
mean more than already
inspiration. Shards of saints & stories blown apart
under fading dust wrappers sky blue cloth fine with no markings or
    annotations to return to.

3.3.3.0

The effect of tidal forces on
time conjectured, unremembered, walk
anyway looking at them
having to live with these memories

& splendour! it does NOT cohere the better for it a lifetime spent
in geometry & falling or falling. Drawing,
direct product of the manifold & a suitable space,
lovely lists of the names of flowers,

refusing all motion & stillness at once all real places
should be or is it will have been
many repetitions / highest apple / tree or fox—
that's what I want rain light rain—

no longer modern for example time & weather
always beginning as ashes begin
directions not a guide not definitive
make a space becoming invisible.

3.3.3.1

One voice or many, one then many
without roots or rooted in a cloud of unknowing only now
spatter, leopard, the starry sky or smallpox scar.
Turn the page. Memory is fire in its cabinet.

No whole these are parts of,
a yellow green ladder trade name Featherlite,
but this room depending how you got here & where you started when
no wristwatches stopped at random times.

A key turning. Plain text. A door.
Watch each thought's trajectory through time as memory ravels round
    itself
electrical demand / power factors / naive presence—
Displacement or caesura the streets all about

& apart of light. History scraped away
can be most easily examined by constructing a manifold
imposed by the desire for order another network
where relativistic effects are important.

3.3.3.2

Cold stars above empty fields. Thick stiff mud. Hoarfrost.
The vanishing of the divergence is not to be regarded as a consequence.
OK, self shatters & the shards are dangerous still.
Sit here with a book. The wind breathes.

Outlines can be enough to be precise.
A path of scatters as before unplanned
breathless & hopeful unbroken distance. Forgetting & retelling
but always another's words the beautiful

story set aside for another jewel green evasion.
Not even one cold full stop of feeling.
I don't know if silence is written by hand.
What grace this leaves us with to be

real & all of it properly radiant life / beautiful desire / gift
flew off silent in the cool of the morning
outside it or coinciding
or prose. Redemption. War. Loss.

3.3.3.3

Less & less let's say the frame shrinks around the clock
fragments & suspicion sometimes an insincere act
sometimes a black white light radiance
& a song even if every note is melancholia or a number,

spatter, leopard, the starry sky or smallpox scar
should be or is it will have been
this close to the end come back to it
grasping in devotion like the raven or kingfisher.

Perhaps forgetting is pure unknowing possible
to be precise. Outlines can be enough
curving / falling / recited / absence
pools of rain & mossy stones, colder, wetter days getting shorter

a roomful of light / a door
into the net of sky / not infinite / receding
remembering clouds & no detail every clock—
The line moves. The shadow moves.

& if I interrupt—

Notes

The construction of the poem

The Absence of Zero consists of 256 16-line poems, and 34 "interruptions."

The structure of the 256 16-line poems is based on the Riemann curvature tensor in 4 dimensions, a mathematical object that describes the curvature of spacetime in Einstein's general relativity. The Riemann curvature tensor is a 4-index tensor with 256 components in 4 dimensions, but various identities result in some of those components always having the value zero; other components are related in various ways so that there are actually only 20 independent components. (See https://mathworld.wolfram.com/RiemannTensor.html for a discussion of this.)

The 16-line poems are of two kinds. There are 112 "nulls," corresponding to the zero-valued components of the Riemann curvature tensor, which are poems where either the first two or last two indices of the poem number (the tensor indices) are the same, for example 0.1.1.1, 2.2.3.1, or 3.3.3.3. Then there are 144 "quartets," which are all the other 16-line poems.

The quartets consist of 4 quatrains. Each quatrain is text drawn from some random page of my original source notebooks. Quatrains may repeat, at random; most do, but some don't. There are a few blank pages in the notebooks: if the random page is blank, the quatrain source text is a random page from S. W. Hawking and G. F. R. Ellis's *The Large Scale Structure of Space-Time.* Each quartet also includes a quotation from one of the 20 sections of T. S. Eliot's *Four Quartets,* reflecting the symmetry of the 20 independent components of the Riemann curvature tensor. This line replaces a randomly selected line in the quartet's 16 lines. Lines drawn from the fourth section of each of Eliot's *Quartets* are repeated, while multiple lines are drawn from the other four sections.

The random numbers generating the quatrains are derived by timing successive pairs of radioactive decays detected by a Geiger-Müller tube interfaced to a computer at https://www.fourmilab.ch/hotbits. This source is a quantum process.

The null poems also have 4 quatrains. Every line comes from a quartet, except for lines that are text drawn at random from C. W. Misner, K. S. Thorne, and J. A. Wheeler's *Gravitation*. The first 16 nulls (that is 0.0.x.y) draw text from Misner, Thorne, and Wheeler, and only the quatrains that are never repeated, of which as it happens there are 81. (There's no reason for that number.) Lines in the null poems that include a time/weather stamp are replaced by some variation of the phrase "time & weather."

The random numbers generating the nulls are derived from atmospheric noise using https://www.random.org/integers. This source is arguably a classical but chaotic process.

The interruptions are a reminder that while general relativity is a classical theory, the real world is a quantum place. This is also reflected in the overlay of randomness on the 16-line poems. The interruptions break in between the quartets at regular intervals, a kind of stutter-step. The number 34 comes from the "magic square" in Albrecht Dürer's etching *Melencolia I:* the numbers in the square add up to 34 along every row, column, and diagonal. The 16 numbers in the magic square are also used as the "section numbers" of the poem: 1 to 16, but a bit out of order. The fact that there is a "hidden" order in those numbers could be thought of as a reference to the idea that quantum mechanics itself might not be fundamental, that there's a deterministic theory of "hidden variables" behind it; the fact that the "magic square" is a piece of medieval hocus-pocus which means nothing could be thought of as a reference to the various proofs that "hidden variables" are actually impossible.

The actual text of each interruption is a random selection of 34 words from the poem "The Wild Fox," which is a kind of commentary on the rest of the poem (and also an elegy) inserted into the middle of the quartets and interruptions, an interruption of an interruption.

The random numbers generating the interruptions are derived from the JavaScript Math.random() function. This is a pseudo-random number generator; both the algorithm and the seed for the generator are determined by the implementation, in this case Chrome.

Sources

Major sources

T. S. Eliot. *The Four Quartets.*

S. W. Hawking and G. F. R. Ellis. *The Large Scale Structure of Space-Time.*

C. W. Misner, K. S. Thorne, and J. A. Wheeler. *Gravitation.*

Quotations from *The Four Quartets* are all in inverted commas.
Quotations from Hawking and Ellis, and Misner, Thorne, and Wheeler,
are not explicitly indicated.

Minor sources

"the mother tongue remains"
> Hannah Arendt. "What Remains? The Language Remains:
> A Conversation with Günter Gaus." (Tr. Joan Stambaugh)

"Clear a space for it" (and others)
> Christina Baillie and Martha Baillie. *Sister Language.*

"A country road. A tree. Evening."
> Samuel Beckett. *Waiting for Godot.*

"Where now? Who now? When now?" (and others)
> Samuel Beckett. *The Unnameable.*

"either the well was very deep or she fell very slowly, for she had plenty of
    time to look about her and to wonder what was going to happen next"
    Lewis Carroll. *Alice's Adventures in Wonderland.*

"my life will shut very beautifully, suddenly"
    E. E. Cummings. "somewhere i have never travelled, gladly beyond."

"Then we came forth to see again the stars."
    Dante. *Inferno.* (Tr. Robert and Jean Hollander)

"Leopard, Starry Sky, Smallpox, Spatter"
    Georges Didi-Huberman. *Atlas, or the Anxious Gay Science.*
    (Tr. Shane Lillis)

"No beginning is the highest truth."
    Diamond Sutra. (Tr. Red Pine)

"You will have to live with these memories and make them / into
    something new"
    T. S. Eliot. *The Cocktail Party.*

"This primarily means that they are not temporally ordered: that time
    does not alter them in any way; and that the notion of time cannot be
    applied to them."
    Sigmund Freud. *Beyond the Pleasure Principle.* (Tr. John Reddick.)

"Not chronologically ordered, not altered by the passage..."
    Sigmund Freud. *The Unconscious.* (Tr. Graham Falkland)

"that the necessity of our geometry cannot be demonstrated"
    Carl Friedrich Gauss. Quoted in Misner, Thorne, and Wheeler.

"Verify the one & disprove the other."

Galileo. Quoted in Misner, Thorne, and Wheeler.

"spread beneath us like a vast constellation"

Daryl Hine. *In & Out.*

"time is irreducibly aporetic"

Joanna Hodge. *Derrida on Time.*

"In lovely blueness"

Friedrich Hölderlin. "In Lieblicher Bläue." (Tr. Michael Hamburger.)

"Loss is something I have. Don't take that away from me."

Ward McBurney. *Sap's War.*

"one of them is fine, and the other one is exquisite."

Ward McBurney. *Sky Train.*

"If this is a diary / is it worthless / like life"

Alice Notley. *Disobedience.*

"mercy & relaxation & even a strength"

Gertrude Stein. *Tender Buttons.*

"home after a long day to feed the cat, like Philip Marlowe"

Wim Wenders and Peter Handke. *Wings of Desire.* (Tr. unknown)

"you that shall cross from shore to shore years hence are more to me, & more in my meditations than you might suppose "

Walt Whitman. "Crossing Brooklyn Ferry."

"What I hold fast to is not one proposition but a nest of propositions."
Ludwig Wittgenstein. *On Certainty*. (Tr. Denis Paul and G. E. M. Anscombe)

"every differentiable symmetry of the action of a physical system has a corresponding conservation law"
Wikipedia: Noether's theorem. Retrieved 2016-02-16.

"a measure of the unpredictability of information content"
Wikipedia: Shannon entropy. Retrieved 2016-04-05.

"cloud cover less than ¾₁₀th at all altitudes"
Wikipedia: Atomic bombings of Hiroshima and Nagasaki. Retrieved 2016-04-02.

The etchings by Albrecht Dürer, *Melencolia I* (1514) and *Saint Jerome in His Study* (1514), are referred to thoughout, and bookend the text itself.

Gerhard Richter's *Cologne Cathedral Window* (2007) and Anselm Kiefer's painting *Die Milchstraße* (1985-87) are also frequently referred to, albeit not by name.

The music and ideas of John Cage are inseparable from the writing of this poem.

"No language stands alone," I wrote near the end of another book. That's more and more true. Thanks to everyone whose works and words, quoted, unquoted, cited, uncited, remembered, and misremembered, form the foundation of *The Absence of Zero*.

Thanks

The date on the first page of the notebook that contains the beginnings of this work is Friday, October 11, 2013. The date on the last page of the seventh, final, notebook with drafts of this work is Friday, April 24, 2020.

Many people helped get from that first date to the last, and from there on to this printed book.

A workshop on the Canadian long poem in winter 2014 provided an occasion to air a very early version. Thanks to the participants in the workshop for their feedback. I concluded the poem wasn't long enough and kept writing.

An earlier version of quartet 3.2.0.1 first appeared in *PRISM international* 56.2 (winter 2018). Thanks to the editors.

Thanks to Kirby at Knife | Fork | Book in Toronto for the opportunity to read a draft of the poem in its entirety in February 2020, and to the audiences who stuck with it for 4 wintry nights. Kirby also later published a version of the interruptions as the chapbook *The Wild Fox*, and has said some nice things about the poem as a whole, for which I'm grateful.

Thanks to Guy Ewing, who has been a constant and supportive reader of the many drafts of this book and other work of mine over the years.

Rose Cullis likewise read, listened, encouraged, and cheered me on when I needed encouragement and cheering on. David Bradford and Aaron Tucker also read drafts, said nice things, and asked good questions.

Special thanks to Margaret Christakos, who wrote a generous and lengthy response to the poem, a small portion of which is excerpted on the back cover.

Steve Zultanski, who edited the book for the press, saw what I was doing and, paying close attention, made it better. Stuart Ross caught more than a few inconsistencies in proofreading. Gareth Lind produced a cover and design that capture the spirit of the poem perfectly. Thanks to you all.

Jay MillAr was interested in this project back in those Long Poem Workshop days, got behind it, and saw it through to the volume you hold in your hands. Given Book*hug's roots in the Canadian experimental poetry world, I can't think of a better publisher for this. Thanks to Jay and Hazel Millar, and everyone at Book*hug, for your work and dedication.

Finally, my debt to both Christina Baillie and Ward McBurney is incalculable. They were early and constant readers of this poem who inspired me to persevere with it again and again, always challenging me with new ways of thinking about, and listening to, language, each in very different ways. Neither Christina nor Ward lived to see *The Absence of Zero* finally finished, but so much of this poem echoes with your missing, much missed voices, my dear friends.

About the Author

R. Kolewe has published two collections of poetry, *Afterletters* (Book*hug, 2014) and *Inspecting Nostalgia* (Talonbooks, 2017), as well as several chapbooks. He lives in Toronto.

Colophon

Manufactured as the first edition of
The Absence of Zero
in the fall of 2021 by Book*hug Press

Edited for the press by Steven Zultanski
Proofread by Stuart Ross
Type and design by Gareth Lind
Typeface: Adobe Caslon Pro and FF Mark
Cover background image: iStock/The7Dew
Printed in Canada

bookhugpress.ca